TEN YEARS OF POP MUSIC

1990-2000

REMEMBERING THE '90s

D0618721

**THE IVORY PALACE
745 N. STATE ST.
UKIAH, CA 95482
(707) 462-8863**

Project Manager: Carol Cuellar
Art Design: Jorge Paredes
Text By: Fucini Productions, Inc.

CONTENTS

Title	Artist	Page

CONTENTS

Title	Artist	Page

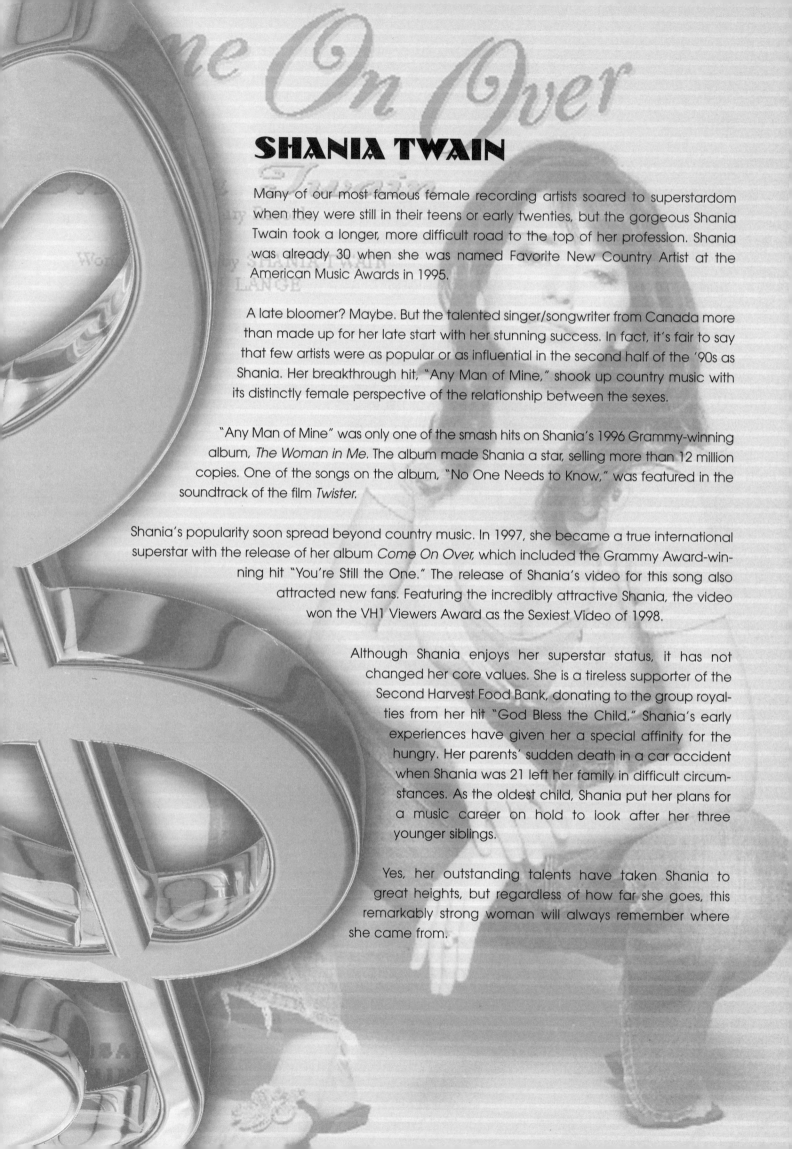

SHANIA TWAIN

Many of our most famous female recording artists soared to superstardom when they were still in their teens or early twenties, but the gorgeous Shania Twain took a longer, more difficult road to the top of her profession. Shania was already 30 when she was named Favorite New Country Artist at the American Music Awards in 1995.

A late bloomer? Maybe. But the talented singer/songwriter from Canada more than made up for her late start with her stunning success. In fact, it's fair to say that few artists were as popular or as influential in the second half of the '90s as Shania. Her breakthrough hit, "Any Man of Mine," shook up country music with its distinctly female perspective of the relationship between the sexes.

"Any Man of Mine" was only one of the smash hits on Shania's 1996 Grammy-winning album, *The Woman in Me*. The album made Shania a star, selling more than 12 million copies. One of the songs on the album, "No One Needs to Know," was featured in the soundtrack of the film *Twister*.

Shania's popularity soon spread beyond country music. In 1997, she became a true international superstar with the release of her album *Come On Over*, which included the Grammy Award-winning hit "You're Still the One." The release of Shania's video for this song also attracted new fans. Featuring the incredibly attractive Shania, the video won the VH1 Viewers Award as the Sexiest Video of 1998.

Although Shania enjoys her superstar status, it has not changed her core values. She is a tireless supporter of the Second Harvest Food Bank, donating to the group royalties from her hit "God Bless the Child." Shania's early experiences have given her a special affinity for the hungry. Her parents' sudden death in a car accident when Shania was 21 left her family in difficult circumstances. As the oldest child, Shania put her plans for a music career on hold to look after her three younger siblings.

Yes, her outstanding talents have taken Shania to great heights, but regardless of how far she goes, this remarkably strong woman will always remember where she came from.

CHRISTINA AGUILERA

When you wish for something and rub a lantern, a genie is supposed to make your dreams come true. Christina Aguilera's storybook rise to superstardom conjures up visions of this kind of magic. In 1999 the first single by this vivacious teenager, "Genie in a Bottle," zoomed to the top of the pop charts. Soon fans throughout the world were not only singing Christina's tunes, but they were also imitating the dazzling moves of her genie dance.

Packing a million watts of charisma in an attractive petite frame, the five-foot-tall Christina is pure magic on stage. Not long ago, Christina made one of her first major international appearances at the Golden Stag Festival in Europe. In a program that included established stars like Sheryl Crow and Diana Ross, the confident teen electrified the big crowd with her singing and dancing, leaving the audience screaming for encore after encore.

Upon her return to the United States, Christina auditioned for the chance to record "Reflection" for the animated film *Mulan*. Her beautiful voice quickly won over the film's producers. Within a week, Christina was in a Los Angeles studio recording "Reflection." *Mulan* premiered in June 1998, and Christina did a TV tour to promote the film, performing her sweetly evocative version of "Reflection" on programs like "CBS This Morning" and "The Donny & Marie Show."

It's fitting that Christina's first big hit came out of the film *Mulan*. Like the lead character in that movie, Christina is a strong and intelligent young woman determined to live out her dreams. Growing up in the Pittsburgh, Pennsylvania area, Christina always knew she wanted to be a singer. Her first "performance" was at a family pool party when she was six. From that point on, the little girl with the big voice was hooked on performing. At the age of ten, she became the youngest person to sing the National Anthem at a Pittsburgh Steelers football game.

Christina's talent has continued to blossom through her teen years. Her incredible range and diversity was evident in her debut album. From the high-power dance tune "Genie in a Bottle" to the soulful strains of "So Emotional," this teen star has shown that her magic knows no boundaries.

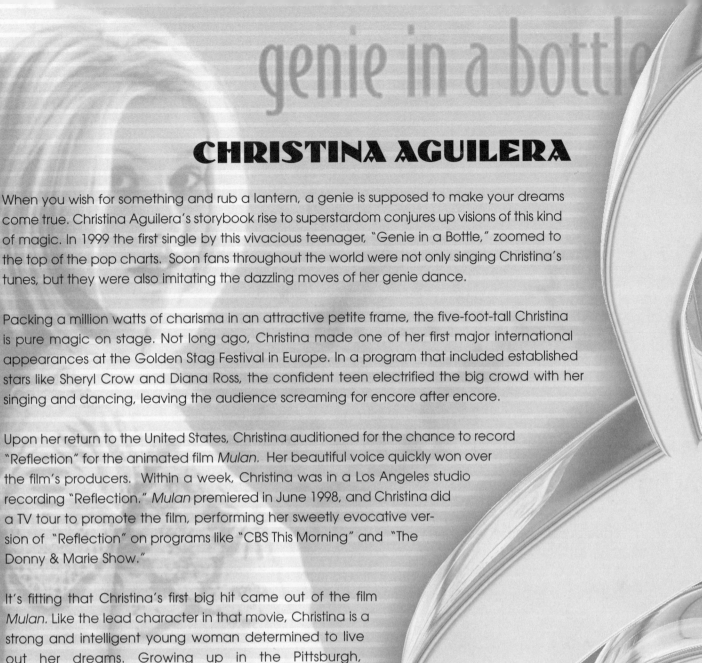

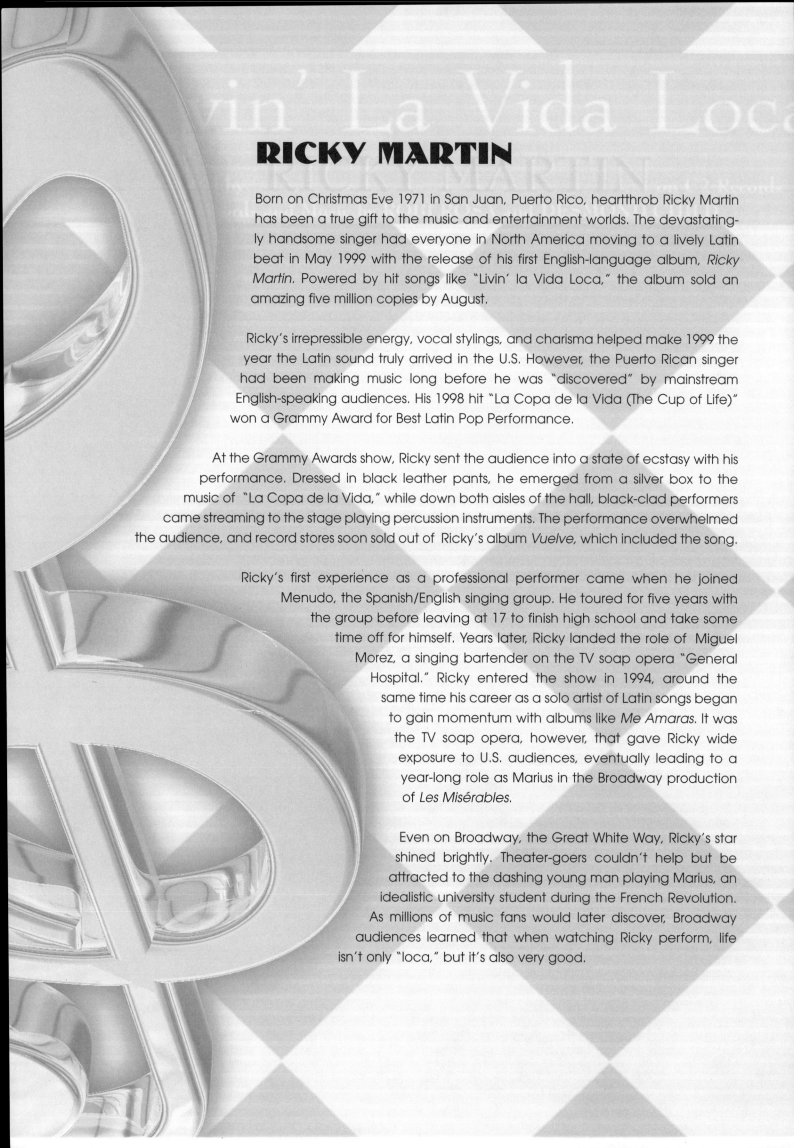

RICKY MARTIN

Born on Christmas Eve 1971 in San Juan, Puerto Rico, heartthrob Ricky Martin has been a true gift to the music and entertainment worlds. The devastatingly handsome singer had everyone in North America moving to a lively Latin beat in May 1999 with the release of his first English-language album, *Ricky Martin.* Powered by hit songs like "Livin' la Vida Loca," the album sold an amazing five million copies by August.

Ricky's irrepressible energy, vocal stylings, and charisma helped make 1999 the year the Latin sound truly arrived in the U.S. However, the Puerto Rican singer had been making music long before he was "discovered" by mainstream English-speaking audiences. His 1998 hit "La Copa de la Vida (The Cup of Life)" won a Grammy Award for Best Latin Pop Performance.

At the Grammy Awards show, Ricky sent the audience into a state of ecstasy with his performance. Dressed in black leather pants, he emerged from a silver box to the music of "La Copa de la Vida," while down both aisles of the hall, black-clad performers came streaming to the stage playing percussion instruments. The performance overwhelmed the audience, and record stores soon sold out of Ricky's album *Vuelve,* which included the song.

Ricky's first experience as a professional performer came when he joined Menudo, the Spanish/English singing group. He toured for five years with the group before leaving at 17 to finish high school and take some time off for himself. Years later, Ricky landed the role of Miguel Morez, a singing bartender on the TV soap opera "General Hospital." Ricky entered the show in 1994, around the same time his career as a solo artist of Latin songs began to gain momentum with albums like *Me Amaras.* It was the TV soap opera, however, that gave Ricky wide exposure to U.S. audiences, eventually leading to a year-long role as Marius in the Broadway production of *Les Misérables.*

Even on Broadway, the Great White Way, Ricky's star shined brightly. Theater-goers couldn't help but be attracted to the dashing young man playing Marius, an idealistic university student during the French Revolution. As millions of music fans would later discover, Broadway audiences learned that when watching Ricky perform, life isn't only "loca," but it's also very good.

foolish game

JEWEL

How much would you pay for a front-row seat at a Jewel concert? A lot of people in San Diego can remember when the privilege of enjoying this poetic genius up close cost only three dollars. That's how much InnerChange, a coffee house in Pacific Beach, charged for Jewel's regular Thursday-night performances in 1993.

Music-lovers crammed into the club for Jewel's four-hour sets. Between songs, the 19-year-old shared stories of her young life with her audience—and what an interesting life it had already been. Jewel Kilcher grew up in Alaska, spending part of her youth on an 800-acre homestead in the village of Homer. She started performing in public at six, when she yodeled in shows put on for tourists. When not on stage, Jewel was a pensive young woman who enjoyed keeping a journal and caring for her horse Clearwater.

After graduating from high school in 1992, Jewel moved to San Diego to pursue a career in music. Her road to stardom was swift but not easy. For a time, Jewel tried to support herself with a variety of jobs, including waitressing, but nothing seemed to fit. Out of money, she left her apartment and lived in a van. Some aspiring musicians might have given up at this point, but Jewel continued to press forward. Soon she met singer/songwriter Steve Poltz, who introduced her to the local music scene.

Jewel's popularity quickly spread beyond San Diego. In late 1993, the wistful 19-year-old, who only months earlier had called a van home, signed a record contract. Less than two years later, Jewel's album *Pieces of You* was released. Featuring songs like "Who Will Save Your Soul," "You Were Meant for Me," and "Foolish Games," the album reached No. 4 on the Billboard 200.

In 1998, Jewel released her second hit album, *Spirit.* She also published her first book of poetry, *A Night Without Armor,* which became a fixture on *The New York Times* bestseller list. Like her original songs, Jewel's poetry shows her incredible gift for conveying complex and subtle feelings in simple yet moving language. Fortunately for us, there is one simple word that has never entered this gifted writer's vocabulary—quit.

ALANIS MORISSETTE

Can lightning strike twice? It certainly has in Alanis Morissette's life. The charismatic Canadian was already a star in her country before she celebrated her seventeenth birthday. Her debut album, *Alanis*, a collection of dance tunes released in 1991, went platinum in Canada, earning her a Juno Award (the country's version of the Grammy) as the Most Promising Female Vocalist. However, a second dance album, *Now Is the Time*, which was released before she graduated from high school, sold only half as well as her debut recording.

At this point, it seemed Alanis might become one of those teen sensations whose careers never survive into their twenties. Then came the second lightning strike. And this time the "bolt" not only electrified Canada, but it also shook up the entire music world.

Moving to Los Angeles after high school, Alanis discarded her original dance sound to pursue an edgier, more intensely personal style of music. In 1995, her now-legendary album *Jagged Little Pill* was released. Powered by hits like "Hand in My Pocket" and "Ironic," the album shattered every sales record in sight. *Jagged Little Pill* has sold an astounding 35 million copies worldwide. Soundscan named *Jagged Little Pill* the best-selling album of the '90s in the U.S.

Following *Jagged Little Pill,* Alanis was showered with awards, including Grammys for Album of the Year, Best Female Rock Vocal Performance, Best Rock Song, and Best Rock Album. She was also named the Most Downloaded Artist on the World Wide Web by Excite.com. Her widely anticipated 1998 album, *Supposed Former Infatuation Junkie,* was another multi-platinum album, with hits like "Thank U" and "So Pure."

In November 1999, Alanis received international praise for her unplugged special on MTV. Appearing on a simple set at the Brooklyn Academy of Music in New York, she gave a heartfelt acoustic performance of her own songs as well as those by other writers. The teen diva of 1991, with her MIDI machines and mixers, had grown into a mature artist, capable of captivating an audience of millions with nothing more than her raw creative power. As Alanis would say, "Isn't it ironic?"

BACKSTREET BOYS

At one time, the Backstreet Boys were the most famous unknowns in the U.S. In 1995–96, the five young guys from Orlando, Florida, were instantly recognizable superstars in Europe and Asia, but whenever they returned to the U.S., BSB members A.J. McLean, Howie Dorough, Nick Carter, Kevin Richardson, and Brian Littrell could have walked down any street without being noticed.

Formed by a group of high school and junior high school students in 1993, BSB played throughout Florida, sometimes opening for stars like Brandy. In 1995, the group released "We've Got It Goin' On." The song wasn't noticed in the U.S., but it took off like a rocket in Europe.

Europeans responded to BSB's strong harmonies and their unique blend of R&B and pop. The group won a Smash Hits Award in London for Best New Tour Act, and they got to play their hit "I'll Never Break Your Heart" on "Top of the Pops." German TV viewers voted BSB the Number One International Group. Austrians made the boys' "I'll Never Break Your Heart" number one on their charts.

By the time the Backstreet Boys released their self-titled debut album in April 1996, the whole world was abuzz—except the U.S. That summer, BSB sold out a 57-date tour of Europe. Later, their up-tempo sound made them the rage of Asia and Australia too. The five-some capped off 1996 by winning the MTV Europe Viewers Choice Award. Then came the conquest of Canada, where BSB sold out 32 shows in less than 20 minutes.

Finally, America was ready for its home-grown superstars. Back in Orlando in 1997, the boys worked on new songs and continued to develop as musicians. By 1998, BSB mania had swept the 50 states, and it has shown no signs of letting up since. The group's Millennium U.S. tour sold out in less than an hour. Within one week of its release, BSB's Millennium album sold more than one million copies. In 1999, when the group held a press conference at MTV's Times Square studios, the crowds became so large that police had to ask the boys to move away from the windows to control the excitement level. The group that left the U.S. as virtual unknowns had come home—and American fans welcomed BSB with open arms and screaming adulation.

BRYAN ADAMS

Canadian-born rocker Bryan Adams has gone to the movies quite often in the '90s, not necessarily as a fan, but as the artist behind some of the decade's most memorable soundtracks. Bryan made his first foray into film music in 1991 when he co-wrote and recorded "(Everything I Do) I Do It for You" for the film *Robin Hood: Prince of Thieves,* starring Kevin Costner. The sweetly haunting song was No. 1 on the Billboard charts for seven straight weeks and earned Bryan a Grammy Award and an Academy Award nomination. In England, the song was even a bigger hit, camping out for 18 weeks at the No. 1 spot, longer than any other recording in the history of British music!

Bryan returned to the movies (and to No. 1 on the charts) again in 1993 with "All for Love," a song he recorded with Sting and Rod Stewart for the film *The Three Musketeers.* That same year, he released a Top-10 hits album that sold more than 13 million copies internationally. The fair-haired rocker then went on an 18-month world tour that took him through Modena, Italy, hometown of Luciano Pavarotti. Bryan and the great tenor performed an Italian version of his hit "Please Forgive Me," which was released on CD.

Following his tour, Bryan was back in the movies again. Audiences who went to see the film *Don Juan DeMarco* in 1995 enjoyed his distinctive voice in the song "Have You Ever Really Loved a Woman?" Like Bryan's other songs for the cinema, this recording rocketed to No. 1 on the Billboard charts, a position it held for five weeks. The powerfully evocative song also earned Bryan his second Academy Award nomination. For the next three years, Bryan stayed away from movie soundtracks and instead released three hit albums: *18 'Til I Die* (1996), *MTV Unplugged* (1997), and *On a Day Like Today* (1998).

During his illustrious career, Bryan has sold more than 55 million albums and seen his hits reach No. 1 status in more than 30 countries. That's quite an accomplishment for a guy who, before launching his recording career, was washing dishes at a Canadian diner. In fact, it's the kind of dream-come-true tale that would be perfect for the movies—and we know the perfect artist to do the theme song.

SARAH McLACHLAN

She's recognized as one of today's most original artist-songwriters, but Sarah McLachlan's impact on the music world goes beyond her own evocative songs. Sarah was the driving force behind the Lilith Fair, the wildly popular all-female traveling summer music festival that debuted in 1997. Playing to sold-out crowds from coast to coast, the Lilith Fair has served not only as a showcase for talented female superstars like Sarah but also as a springboard to help lesser-known women gain national recognition.

Sarah's dedication to creating a festival that would help up-and-coming artists, after she herself had already reached superstar status, typifies her generous, giving spirit. This open and caring outlook on life is reflected in Sarah's music, with songs like the ethereal and haunting "I Will Remember You" and "Sweet Surrender." Another song, "Hold On," from Sarah's 1994 album Fumbling Toward Ecstasy, was inspired by the story of a woman whose fiancé discovers he has AIDS. This song later appeared on *No Alternative*, a compilation album put together to raise money for AIDS research.

The innovative and generous artist from Halifax, Nova Scotia, was just three when she got her first instrument, a ukulele (she was too small for a guitar). Later, Sarah studied classical guitar, piano, and voice. After playing in high school bands, Sarah struck out on her own. In 1988, the then-19-year-old songstress released her first album, *Touch,* which went gold in Canada. International stardom and more albums followed, including *Solace, Surfacing,* and her live concert release *Mirrorball.* In 1999, Sarah received the Billboard Music Award for Best Contemporary Adult Single for her chart-topping ballad "Angel."

Through it all, Sarah has remained down-to-earth and dedicated to friends and personal causes. However, she also confesses to enjoying the glitz of the rock lifestyle. *Mirrorball* was given its name because McLachlan loves performing on stage under spinning silver spotlights called mirror-balls. It's an example of how this passionate and genuine artist doesn't fit into a mold—and why her music will always have a surprising, interesting edge.

ALL 4 LOVE

Lyric and Music by
COLOR ME BADD and
HOWARD THOMPSON

1. I'm so glad you're my girl, I'll do an-y-thing 4_ U.
2. I will nev-er leave U, sug-ar, this I guar-an-tee. I

Call U ev-ery night and give U flow-ers 2.___ I
look in-2 the fu-ture and see U___ and me.___

thank the Lord for U and think a-bout U all the_ time,___ and
Knight in shin-ing ar-mor, I will B your fai-ry_ tale.___ I

All 4 Love - 4 - 1

14

all__ 4 love.__   all,

Spoken: Yo! Come here, sweetheart.
The distance B-tween us,

all,

I want U 2 know something, alright.
an ocean of tears.

all,   all, all,   all, all,   all.

See, every day N my life without U would   *B like a hundred years.*
See, all the things I do 4 U

all.

are 4 love.   *Dig it.*

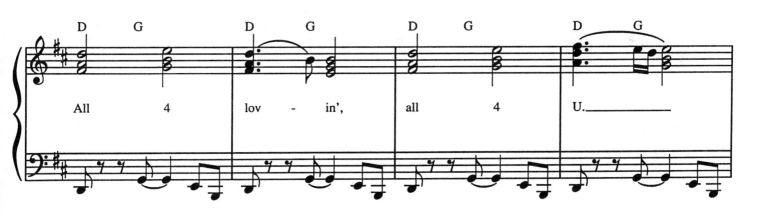

All   4   lov - in',   all   4   U._____

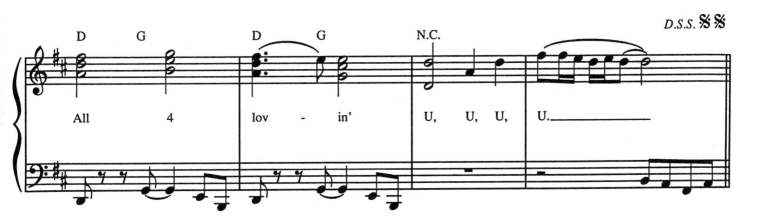

All   4   lov - in'   U,   U,   U,   U._____

ALL I HAVE TO GIVE

Words and Music by
FULL FORCE

18

Chorus:

ALL STAR

Tune guitar down a half step

Words and Music by
GREG CAMP

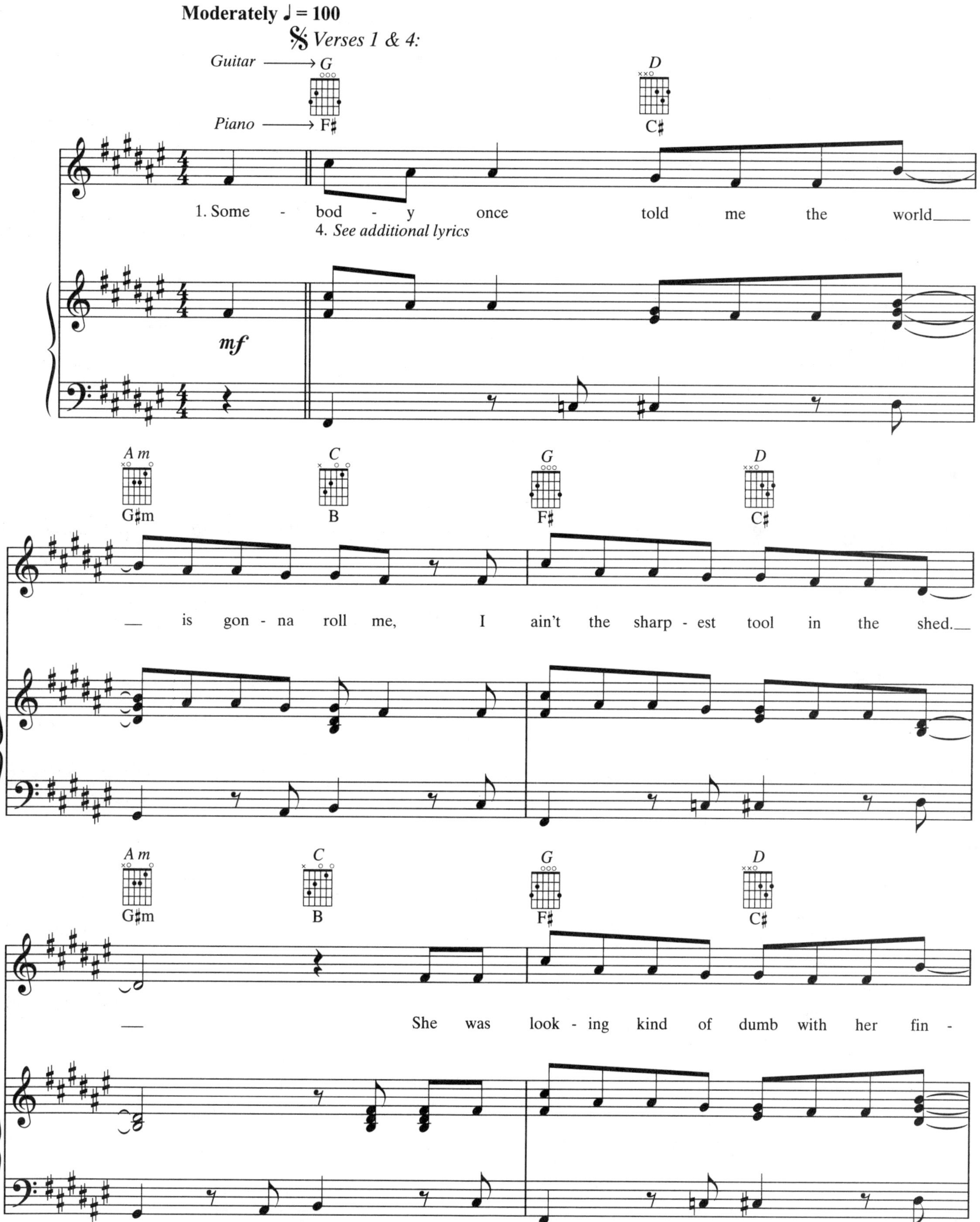

Moderately ♩ = 100

Verses 1 & 4:

1. Some-bod-y once told me the world___
4. *See additional lyrics*

___ is gon-na roll me, I ain't the sharp-est tool in the shed.___

___ She was look-ing kind of dumb with her fin-

All Star - 7 - 1

28

All Star - 7 - 6

Verse 3:
It's a cool place and they say it gets colder.
You're bundled up now, wait till you get older.
But the meteor men beg to differ,
Judging by the hole in the satellite picture.
The ice we skate is getting pretty thin.
The water's getting warm, so you might as well swim.
My world's on fire, how about yours?
That's the way I like it and I'll never get bored.
(To Chorus:)

Verse 4:
Somebody once asked, could I spare some change for gas.
I need to get myself away from this place.
I said, "Yep, what a concept;
I could use a little fuel myself
And we could all use a little change."
(To Verse 5:)

ALWAYS AND FOREVER

Words and Music by
ROD TEMPERTON

32

34

BACK AT ONE

Words and Music by
BRIAN McKNIGHT

Slowly ♩ = 72

Verse:

1. It's un-de-ni - a - ble that we should be_____ to - geth - er.
2. It's so in-cred - i-ble, the way things work_____ them - selves_____ out.

It's un-be-liev - a-ble how I used to say_____ that I'd_____ fall nev - er.
And all e-mo - tion-al, once you know what_____ it's all_____ a - bout,_____ hey.

The ba-sis is need_____ to know. If you don't know just how_____ I feel,_____ then
And un - de-sir - a-ble, for us to be_____ a - part._____ I

ANGEL OF MINE

Words and Music by
RHETT LAWRENCE and TRAVON POTTS

Slowly ♩ = 96

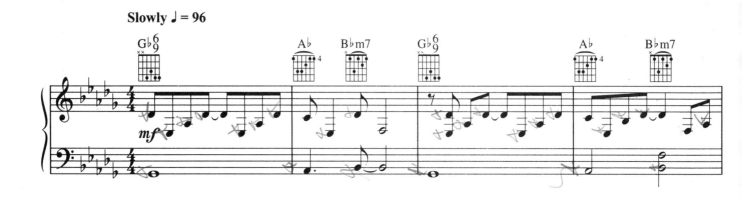

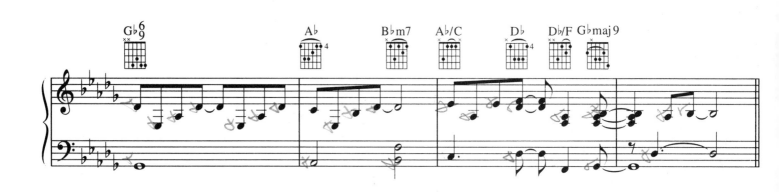

Verse 1:

1. When I first saw you, I al - read - y knew____ there was some-thing

Angel of Mine - 6 - 1

Pre-chorus 1 & 2:

1. How you changed my world, you'll nev-er know.__ I'm dif-f'rent now,__ you
2. What you mean to me, you'll nev-er know.__ Deep in-side__ I

Chorus:

helped me grow._____ } You came in-to my life straight from a-bove.__
need to show._____

When I lost all hope, you showed me love.__ I'm check-ing for you, boy, you're

44

Angel of Mine - 6 - 5

ANY MAN OF MINE

Words and Music by
SHANIA TWAIN and
ROBERT JOHN "MUTT" LANGE

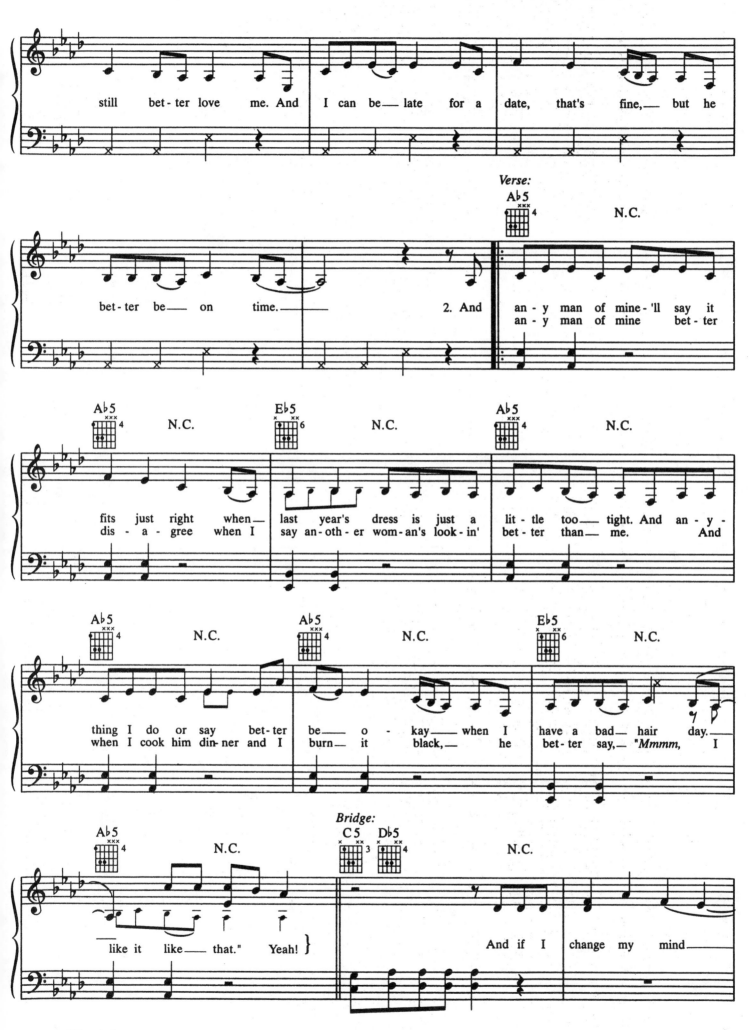

50

Tag:
You gotta shimmy shake, make the earth quake.
Kick, turn, stomp, stomp, then you jump heel to toe, Do Si Do
'Til your boots wanna break, 'til your feet and your back ache
Keep it movin' 'til you just can't take anymore.
Come on, everybody on the floor, a-one two, a-three four.
Hup two, hup if you wanna be a man of mine, that's right.
This is what a woman wants...

From the Motion Picture "REALITY BITES"

BABY, I LOVE YOUR WAY

Words and Music by
PETER FRAMPTON

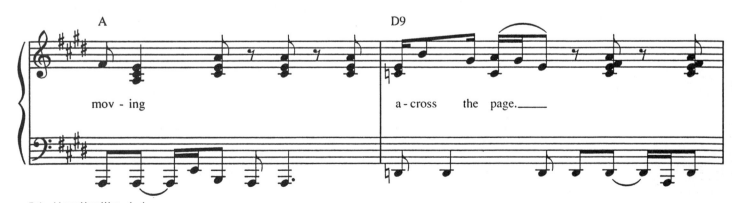

Baby, I Love Your Way - 4 - 1

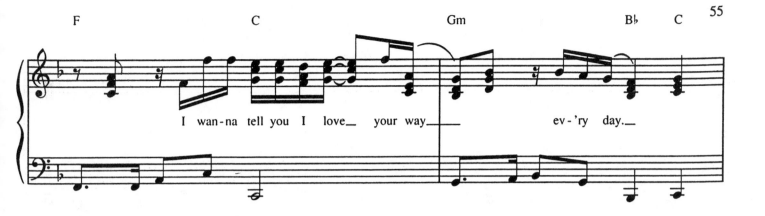

I wan-na tell you I love_ your way._____ ev-'ry day._

I wan-na be with you night_ and day._

Repeat ad lib. and fade

Verse 2:
The moon appears to shine and light the sky
With the help of some fireflies.
I wonder how they have the power to shine;
I can see them under the pine.
(To Bridge:)

Verse 3:
Instrumental solo

Verse 4:
I can see the sunset in your eyes,
Brown and gray and blue besides.
Clouds are stalking islands in the sun.
I wish I could buy one out of season.
(To Bridge:)

BECAUSE YOU LOVED ME
(Theme from "Up Close & Personal")

Words and Music by
DIANE WARREN

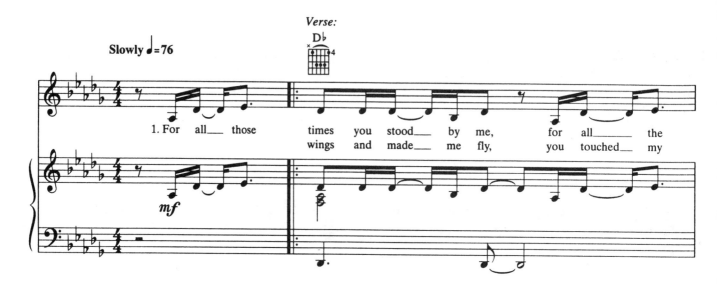

Verse:

Slowly ♩ = 76

1. For all___ those times you stood___ by me, for all___ the
wings and made___ me fly, you touched___ my

truth that you made me see, for all___ the joy you brought to my life,___ for all___ the
hand, I could touch the sky. I lost___ my faith you gave it back to me. You said___ no

wrong that you___ made right, for ev-ery___ dream you made___ come true, for all___ the
star was out___ of reach, you stood___ by___ me and I___ stood tall. I had___ your

60

Because You Loved Me - 5 - 5

BREAKFAST AT TIFFANY'S

Words and Music by
TODD PIPES

Moderately ♩ = 104

1. You'll say___

Verse:

___ see you,___ the on - ly one___ who knew___ me, but
3. You'll say___ we got noth - ing in com - mon, no

we got noth - ing in com - mon, no

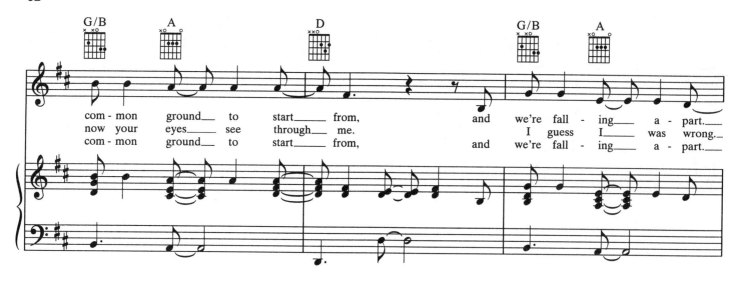

com - mon ground__ to start__ from, and we're fall - ing__ a - part.__
now your eyes__ see through__ me. I guess I__ was wrong.__
com - mon ground__ to start__ from, and we're fall - ing__ a - part.__

You'll say__
So__

what now?__ the world has come__ be - tween__ us, our
You'll say__ the world has come__ be - tween__ us, our

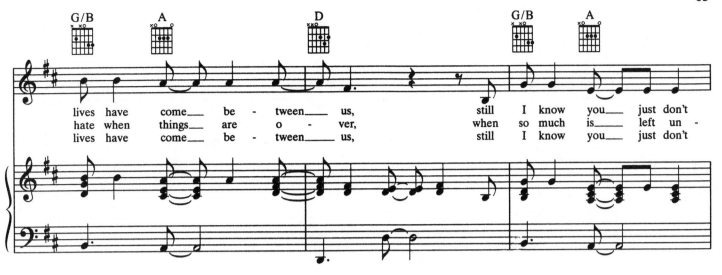

lives have come____ be - tween____ us,   still   I   know   you____ just don't
hate when things____ are   o - ver,   when so much is____ left un -
lives have come____ be - tween____ us,   still   I   know   you____ just don't

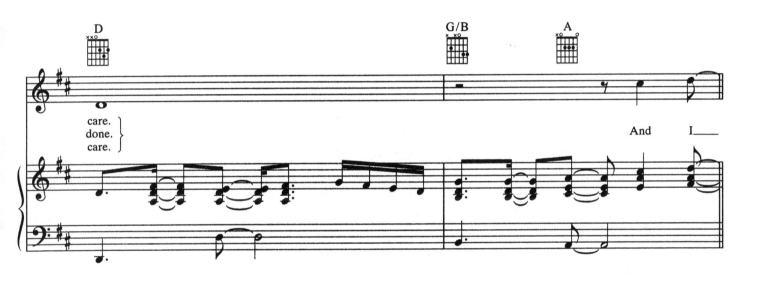

care.
done.
care.

And I____

% Chorus:

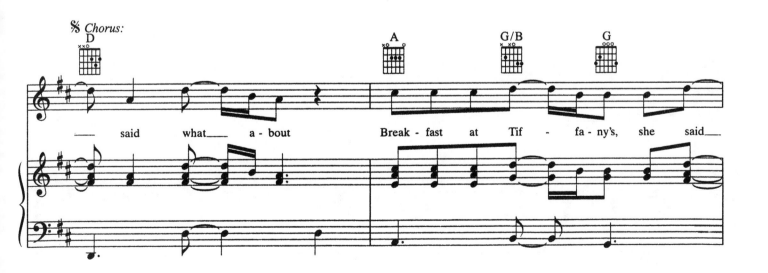

____ said what____ a - bout   Break - fast   at   Tif - fa - ny's,   she   said____

one thing we got._____

Ooh,_____ and I_____

rit.

Breakfast at Tiffany's - 5 - 5

BREATHE

Words and Music by
STEPHANIE BENTLEY
and HOLLY LAMAR

Breathe - 5 - 1

Verses 2 & 3:

2. All my thoughts just seem to set-tle on___ the breeze___
3. In a way, I know my heart___ is wak - ing up___

when I'm ly-in' wrapped___ up in your___ arms.
as all the walls___ come tum-blin'___ down.

The whole world just fades a-way,___ the on - ly thing___ I
Clos-er than I've ev-er felt___ be-fore___ and I know and you know

68

Chorus:

70

BUTTERFLY KISSES

Words and Music by
BOB CARLISLE and RANDY THOMAS

Slowly and tenderly ♩ = 84

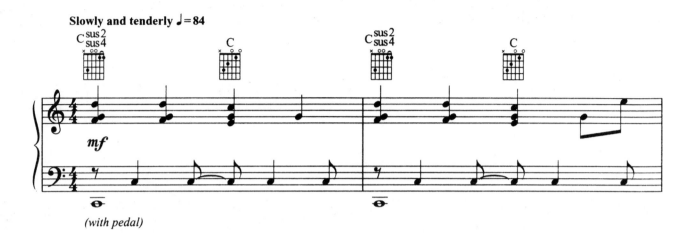

(with pedal)

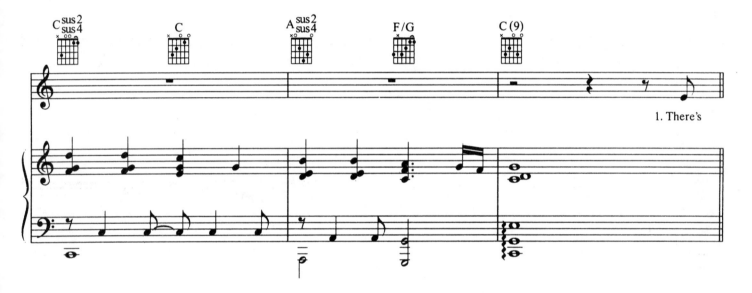

1. There's

%. *Verses 1 & 3:*

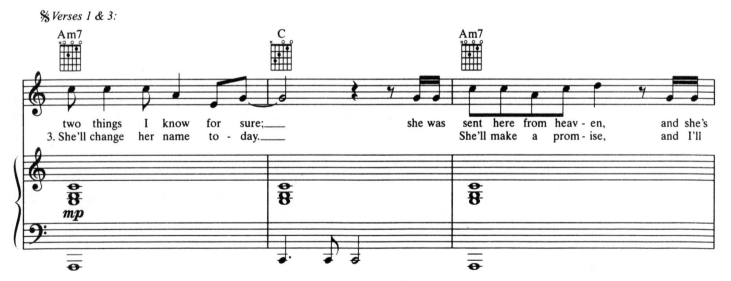

two things   I know   for   sure;___   she was   sent   here   from heav - en,   and she's
3. She'll change   her   name   to - day.___   She'll make   a   prom - ise,   and I'll

Butterfly Kisses - 7 - 1

CHANGE THE WORLD

Words and Music by
TOMMY SIMS, GORDON KENNEDY
and WAYNE KIRKPATRICK

YOU OUGHTA KNOW

Lyrics by
ALANIS MORISSETTE

Music by
ALANIS MORISSETTE and GLEN BALLARD

CONSTANT CRAVING

Words and Music by
k.d. lang and BEN MINK

1. Ev - en through the dark - est phase, be
2. May - be a great mag - net pulls all

D.S. (instrumental)

it thick or thin. _____ Al - ways some-one
souls to - wards truth. _____ Or may - be it is

march - es brave, here be - neath my
life it - self, that feeds wis - dom to its

Constant Craving - 3 - 1

88

CRUSH

Words and Music by
ANDY GOLDMARK, MARK MUELLER,
BERNY COSGROVE and KEVIN CLARK

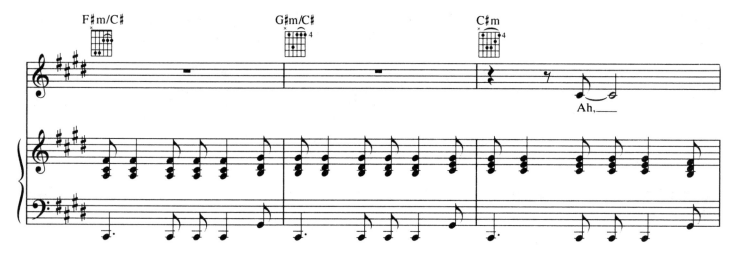

Crush - 5 - 1

'ry-thing I do_____ de-pends on you._____ Sha la____ la la la._____

Sha la____ la la._____ 2. It's

Va - nil - la skies,_____

white____ pick - et fenc - es in_____ your_____ eyes._____

THE CUP OF LIFE
(LA COPA DE LA VIDA)

Words and Music by
ROBI ROSA, LUIS G. ESCOLAR
and DESMOND CHILD

Moderate dance beat ♩ = 108

The Cup of Life - 7 - 1

Go! Go! Gol! A - lé, a - lé, a - lé.

Percussion

G7   Cm   G7   Cm

G7   Cm

100

lla._____ Lu - char_ por e - lla._____ Si! Si! Si!

Tu y yo! A - lé, a - lé, a - lé. Go! Go! Gol! A -

lé, a - lé, a - lé._____ Ar - ri - ba va! El mun-do_es-tá de pie.

Go! Go! Gol! A - lé, a - lé, a - lé._____ lé, a - lé, a - lé._____

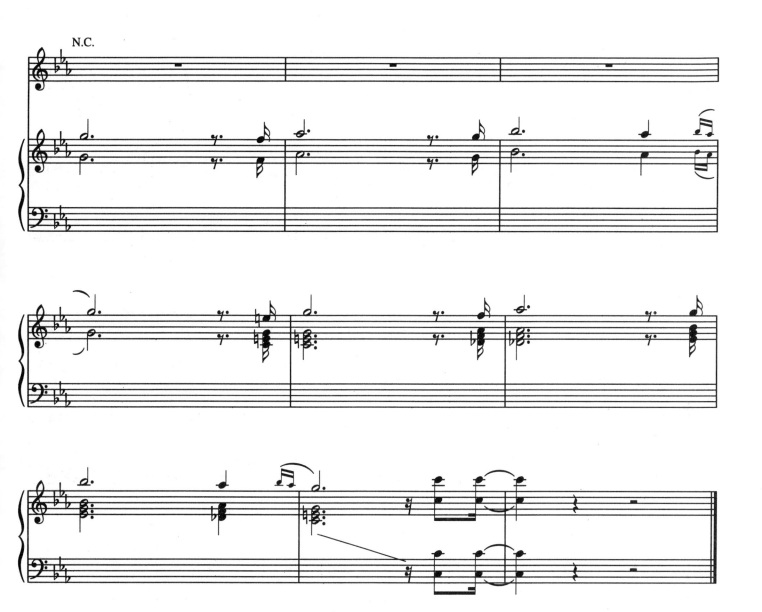

Verso 2:
La vida es competición.
Hay que soñar ser campéon.
La copa es la bendicion.
La canaras, go, go, go.
Tu instinto natural.
Vencer a tu rival.
Tienes que pelear por una estrella.
La copa del amor.
Para sobrevivir y luchar por ella.
Luchar por ella. *(Si!)*
Luchar por ella. *(Si!)*
(Al Coro:)

DO YOU BELIEVE IN US

Words and Music by
JON SECADA and
MIGUEL A. MOREJON

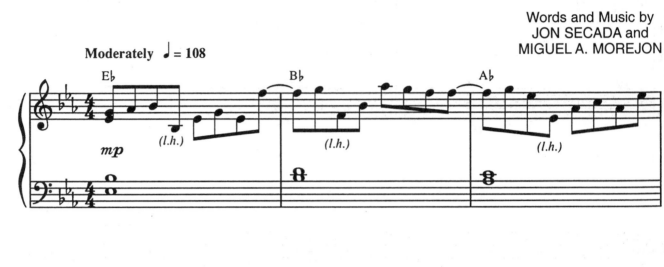

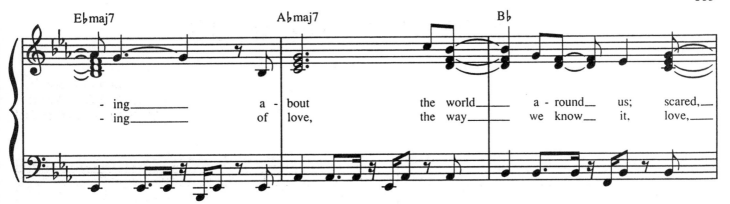

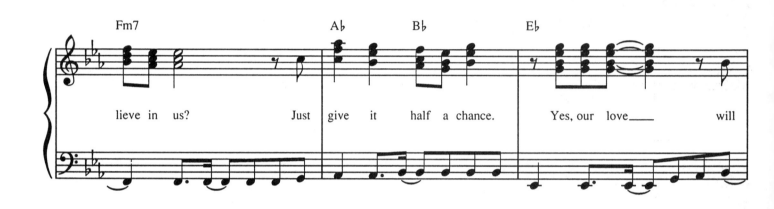

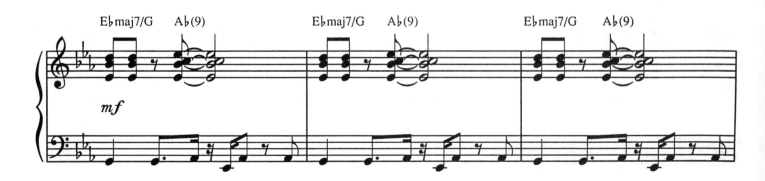

Noth-ing can change__ us; say it's gon-na__ be__ al - right, it's gon-na

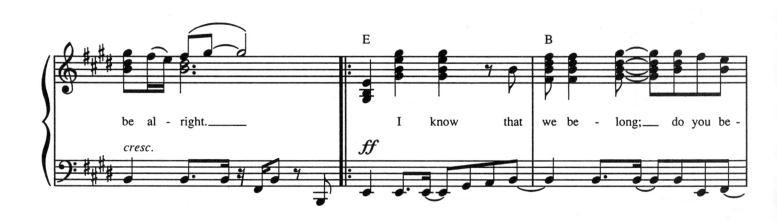

be al - right.____ I know that we be - long;__ do you be-

cresc. ff

lieve in us? Just give it half a chance. Yes, our love____ will

Repeat ad lib. and fade

still be strong;__ girl, I be - lieve in us. I'll give you all I can.

FROM THIS MOMENT ON

Words and Music by
SHANIA TWAIN and R.J. LANGE

From This Moment On - 7 - 1

108

ing   I would-n't   give,_____   from this   mo-ment   on.__

Chorus:

You're the rea-son I__ be-lieve_ in

love._____   And   you're the an-swer to__   my prayers_ from

DON'T CRY FOR ME ARGENTINA

Words by
TIM RICE

Music by
ANDREW LLOYD WEBBER

Don't Cry for Me Argentina - 8 - 1

118

Don't Cry for Me Argentina - 8 - 5

DREAMING OF YOU

Words and Music by
TOM SNOW and
FRANNE GOLDE

1. Late at night when all the world___ is sleep-ing, I stay up and think of you.___ And I

wish on a star___ that some-where you are___ think-ing of me, too.___ 'Cause I'm

Dreaming of You - 6 - 1

Chorus:

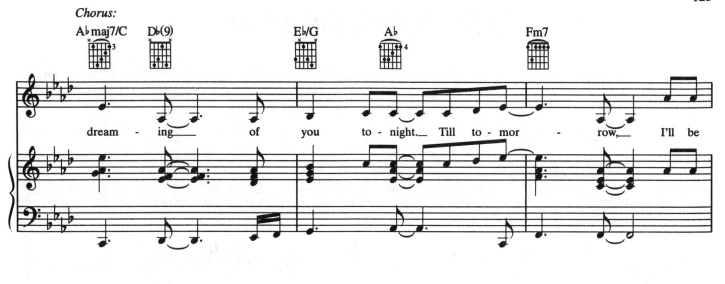

dream - ing of you to - night. Till to - mor - row, I'll be

hold-ing you tight. And there's no - where in the world I'd rath - er be than

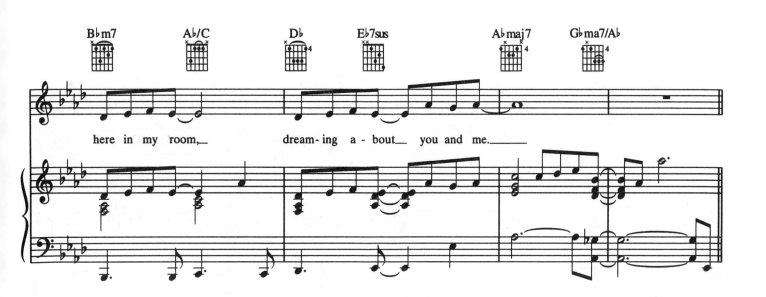

here in my room, dream-ing a - bout you and me.

From the Twentieth Century Fox Motion Picture "ONE FINE DAY"

FOR THE FIRST TIME

Words and Music by
JAMES NEWTON HOWARD,
ALLAN RICH and JUD FRIEDMAN

Slowly ♩ = 62

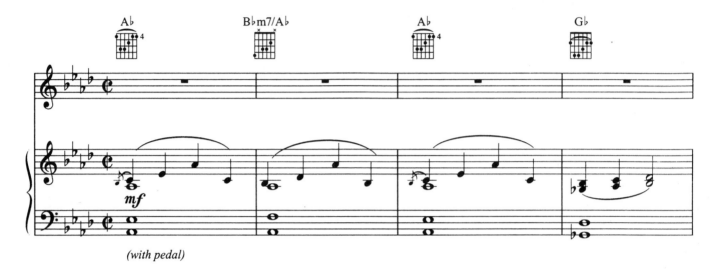

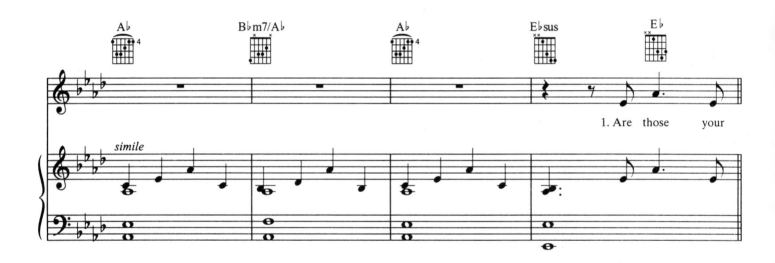

Verse:

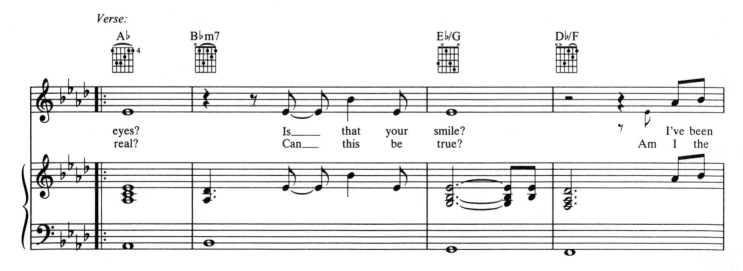

For the First Time - 6 - 1

For the First Time - 6 - 2

132

Chorus:

And for the first time, I am look-ing in____ your eyes.____

For the first time, I'm____ see-ing who you are.____

I can't be-lieve____ how much I see____ when you're look-ing back____ at me.____

FROM A DISTANCE

Lyrics and Music by
JULIE GOLD

Slowly ♩ = 66

with Pedal

Verse:

1. From a dis-tance, the world looks blue and green, and the snow-capped mountains white. From a dis-tance, the o-cean meets the stream, and the ea-gle takes to

From a Distance - 4 - 1

Verse 2:
From a distance, we all have enough,
And no one is in need.
There are no guns, no bombs, no diseases,
No hungry mouths to feed.
From a distance, we are instruments
Marching in a common band;
Playing songs of hope, playing songs of peace,
They're the songs of every man.
(To Bridge:)

Verse 3:
From a distance, you look like my friend
Even though we are at war.
From a distance I just cannot comprehend
What all this fighting is for.
From a distance there is harmony
And it echos through the land.
It's the hope of hopes, it's the love of loves.
It's the heart of every man.

GENIE IN A BOTTLE

Words and Music by
PAMELA SHEYNE, DAVID FRANK
and STEVE KIPNER

Genie in a Bottle - 5 - 1

Chorus:

Genie in a Bottle - 5 - 4

⊕ *Coda*

If you want to be with me, ba - by, there's a price to pay. I'm a ge - nie in a bot-

tle, you got-ta rub me the right way. If you want to be with me, I can make your wish come

true. Just come and set__ me free,_____ ba - by, and I'll be with you.__

I'm a ge - nie in a bot - tle, ba - by, come, come, come on and let me out.

HANDS

Words and Music by
JEWEL KILCHER and PATRICK LEONARD

Hands - 5 - 1

Repeat ad lib. and fade

Hands - 5 - 5

Verse 2:
Poverty stole your golden shoes,
It didn't steal your laughter.
And heartache came to visit me,
But I knew it wasn't ever after.
We'll fight not out of spite,
For someone must stand up for what's right.
'Cause where there's a man who has no voice,
There ours shall go on singing.
(To Chorus:)

HAND IN MY POCKET

Lyrics by
ALANIS MORISSETTE

Music by
ALANIS MORISSETTE and GLEN BALLARD

Hand in My Pocket - 4 - 1

high but I'm ground-ed,   I'm sane but I'm o-ver-whelmed,   I'm
care but I'm rest-less,   I'm here but I'm real-ly __ gone,   I'm
sad but I'm laugh-ing,   I'm brave but I'm chick-en __ shit,   I'm

lost but I'm hope-ful, ba-by.   What it all comes down __
wrong and I'm sor-ry, ba-by.   What it all comes down __
                        Solo ends What it all comes down __
sick but I'm pret-ty, ba-by.   What it all boils down __

G5/F   Csus2

__ to   is that ev-'ry-thing's gon-na be
__ to   is that ev-'ry-thing's gon-na be
__ to   is that I have-n't got it all fig-ured
__ to   is that no one's real-ly got it fig-ured

G5

fine, fine, fine. _____   I've got
quite al-right. _____   I've got
out just yet. _____   I've got
out just yet. _____   I've got

Hand in My Pocket - 4 - 2

one hand in my pock - et   and the oth - er one is giv - ing a high five.
one hand in my pock - et   and the oth - er one is flick - ing a cig - a - rette.
one hand in my pock - et   and the oth - er one is giv - ing the peace sign.
one hand in my pock - et   and the oth - er one is play - ing the pi - an - o.

To Coda ⊕

I feel

D.S. al Coda

I'm

CODA

And what it all comes down ___ to, my ___ friends,   yeah, ___

From the Original Motion Picture Soundtrack "DON JUAN DeMARCO"

HAVE YOU EVER REALLY LOVED A WOMAN?

Lyrics by
BRYAN ADAMS and
ROBERT JOHN "MUTT" LANGE

Music by
MICHAEL KAMEN

Have You Ever Really Loved a Woman? - 6 - 1

154

She will be there for you, tak-ing good care__ of you.__ You real-ly got-ta *love__your wom-an.__*

(Instrumental solo . . .

And when you

. . . end solo)

find your-self ly-ing help-less in__ her arms,_____ you know you real-ly

tell me, have you ev-er real - ly, real-ly, real-ly ev-er loved_ a wom-an?_____ So

tell me, have you ev-er real - ly, real-ly, real-ly ev-er loved_ a wom-an? Oh, just

tell me, have you ev - er real - ly, real - ly, real - ly ev - er loved_____ a

wom - an?_____

HERE AND NOW

Words and Music by
TERRY STEELE and
DAVID ELLIOTT

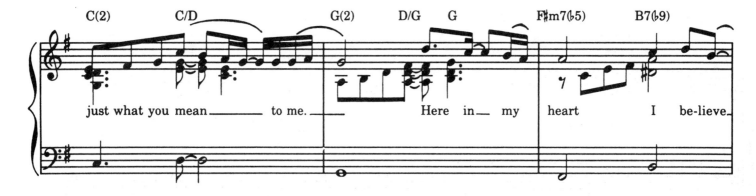

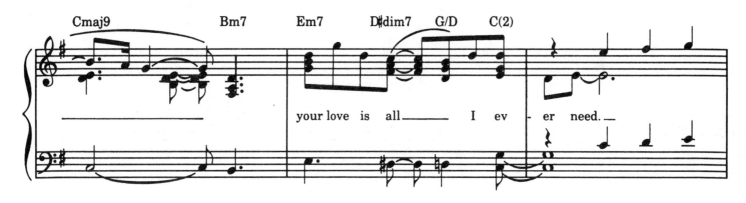

Here and Now - 4 - 1

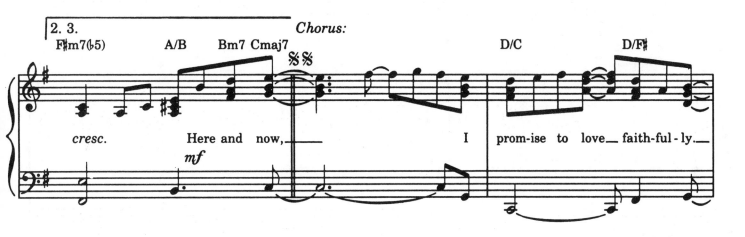

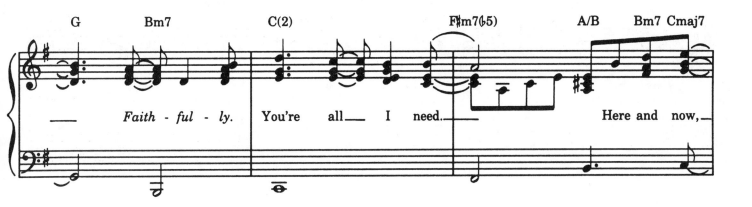

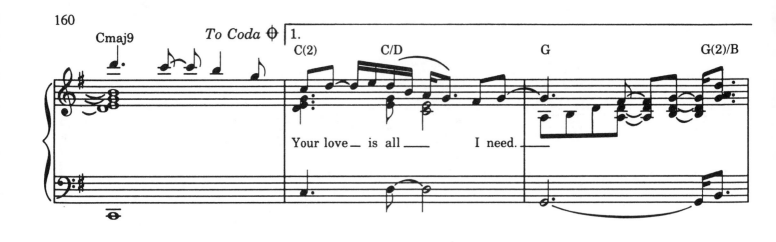

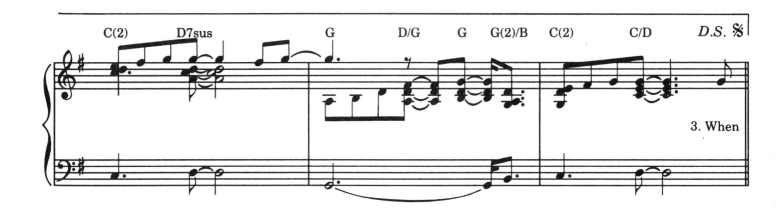

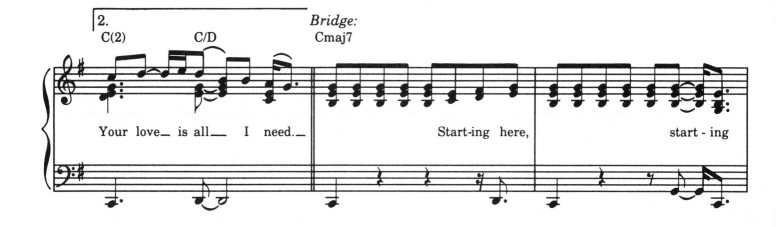

Verse 2:
I look in your eyes and there I see
What happiness really means.
The love that we share makes life so sweet,
Together we'll always be.
This pledge of love feels so right,
And ooh, I need you.
To Chorus:

Verse 3:
When I look in your eyes, there I see
All that a love should really be.
And I need you more and more each day,
Nothing can take your love away.
More than I dare to dream,
I need you.
To Chorus:

I CAN SEE CLEARLY NOW

Words and Music by
JOHNNY NASH

I Can See Clearly Now - 3 - 2

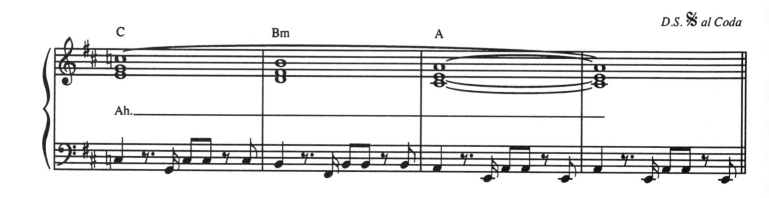

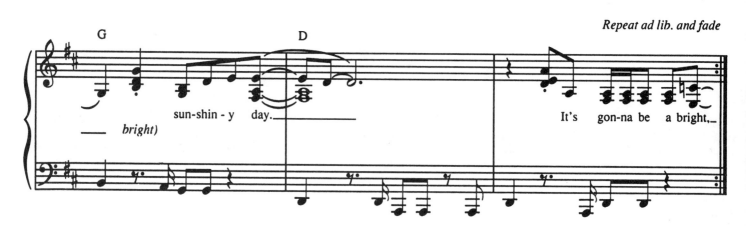

Verse 3:
I can see clearly now, the rain is gone.
I can see all obstacles in my way.
Here is that rainbow I've been praying for,
It's gonna be a bright, bright sunshiny day.
It's gonna be a bright, bright sunshiny day.

I DO (CHERISH YOU)

Words and Music by
KEITH STEGALL and DAN HILL

*Enharmonic chord labeling of F♭maj7.

I Do (Cherish You) - 5 - 1

Verse 2:
In my world before you,
I lived outside my emotions.
Didn't know where I was going
Till that day I found you.
How you opened my life
To a new paradise.
In a world torn by change,
Still with all of my heart,
Till my dying day . . .
(To Chorus:)

From the Motion Picture "Robin Hood: Prince Of Thieves"

(EVERYTHING I DO) I DO IT FOR YOU

Lyrics and Music by
BRYAN ADAMS, ROBERT JOHN LANGE
and MICHAEL KAMEN

Slowly ♩ = 66

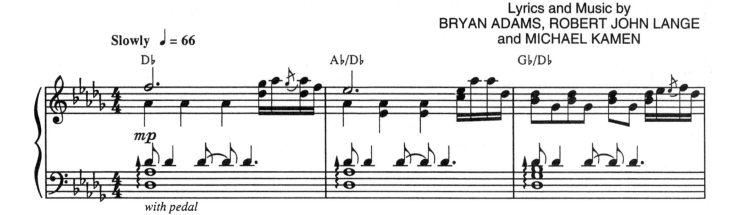

(Everything I Do) I Do It for You - 5 - 1

sac - ri - fice. Don't tell me it's not worth fight-ing for. I can't

help it, there's noth-ing I want more. You know it's true,____ ev-ery-thing I_

_ do,____ I do it for____ you.____ There's

no love____ like your love,____ and no__ oth - er could give

more ___ love. There's no - where ___ un - less you're ___ there, all the

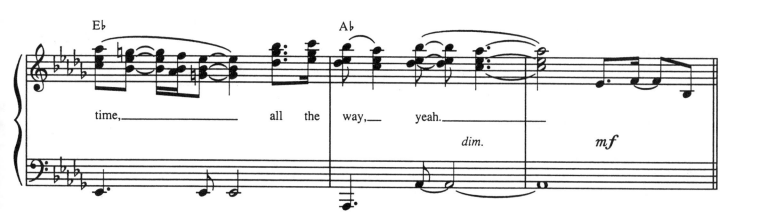

time, ___ all the way, ___ yeah. ___
dim. *mf*

(instrumental solo . . .

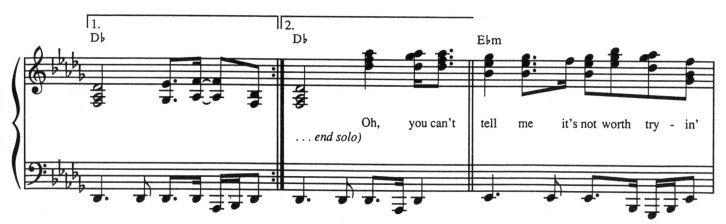

1. 2.

Oh, you can't tell me it's not worth try - in'
. . . end solo)

for.___ I can't help___ it, there's noth-ing I want more. Yeah,_ I would

cresc. *f*

fight_ for you,___ I'd lie___ for you,___ walk the wire___ for you,___ yeah,_ I'd

die for_ you._____ You know it's true, ev-ery-thing I_

dim. *mp*

_ do,___ oh,___ I do it for___ you.___

rit. *dim.* *p*

I SEE YOUR SMILE

Words and Music by
JON SECADA and
MIGUEL A. MOREJON

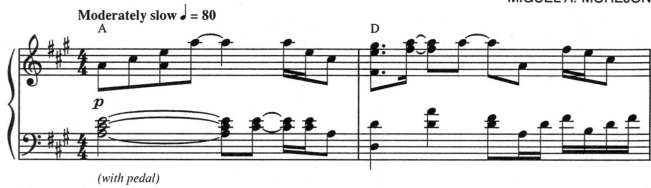

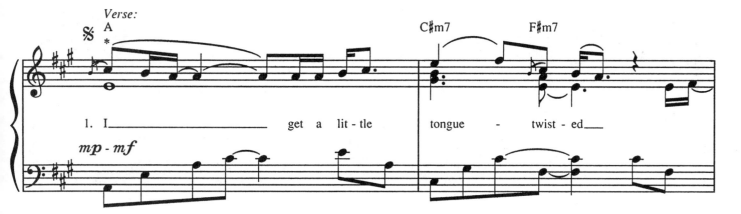

Melody is sung one octave lower.
I See Your Smile - 5 - 1

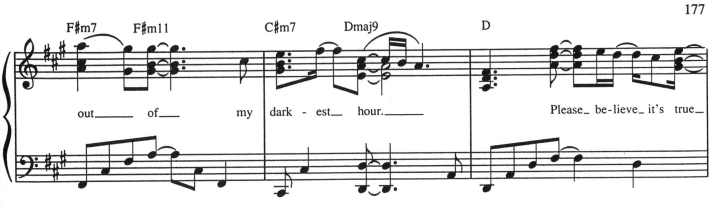

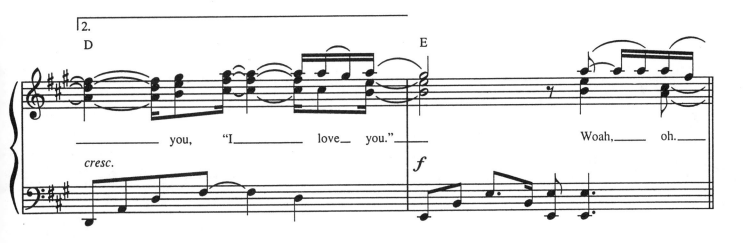

Verse 2:
I've taken too many chances,
Searching for the truth in love that's in my heart.
Tell me if I've made the wrong advances;
Tell me if I've made you feel ashamed.
'Cause I know I have to do this;
Would you hold my hand right through it?
(To Chorus:)

I WANT TO COME OVER

Words and Music by
MELISSA ETHERIDGE

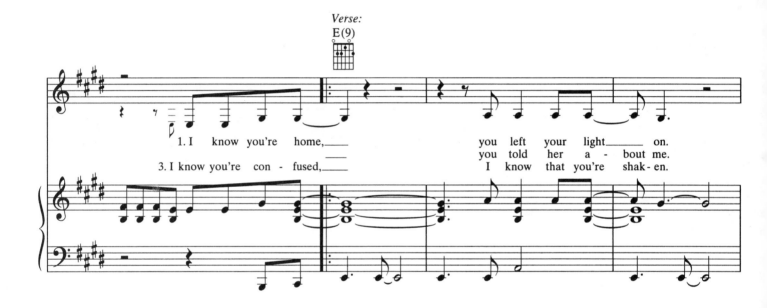

1. I know you're home,___ you left your light____ on.
you told her a - bout me.
3. I know you're con - fused,___ I know that you're shak - en.

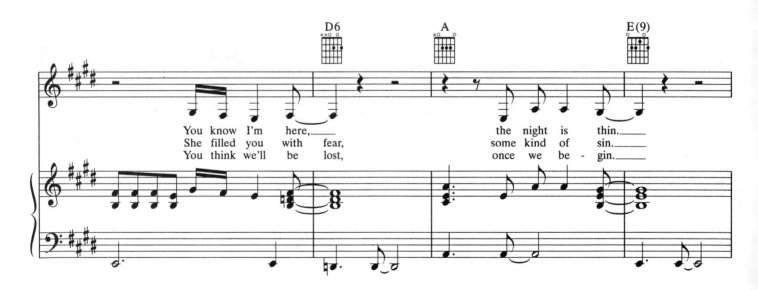

You know I'm here,___ the night is thin.___
She filled you with fear, some kind of sin.___
You think we'll be lost, once we be - gin.___

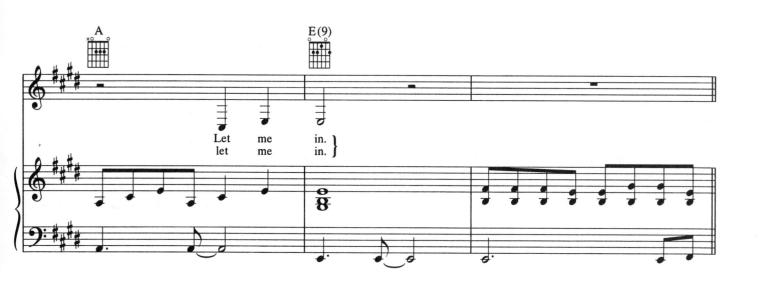

I Want to Come Over - 6 - 4

184

I Want to Come Over - 6 - 5

I WILL ALWAYS LOVE YOU

Words and Music by
DOLLY PARTON

Verse 1:
1. If I should stay, I would only be in your way. So I'll go, but I know I'll think of you ev'ry step of the way. And

Chorus:
I will always love you.

I will always love you.

I Will Always Love You - 5 - 1

188

I Will Always Love You - 5 - 3

Verse 3: Instrumental solo

Verse 4:
I hope life treats you kind
And I hope you have all you've dreamed of.
And I wish to you, joy and happiness.
But above all this, I wish you love.
(To Chorus:)

IF IT MAKES YOU HAPPY

Words and Music by
SHERYL CROW and JEFF TROTT

If It Makes You Happy - 5 - 1

192

If it makes you hap - py,___ then why the hell are you so___ sad?

3.We've been far,___

I WILL COME TO YOU

Words and Music by
ISAAC HANSON, TAYLOR HANSON,
ZACHARY HANSON, BARRY MANN
and CYNTHIA WEIL

197

I Will Come to You - 6 - 2

I Will Come to You - 6 - 6

From The Fox Searchlight Film, "THE BROTHERS McMULLEN"

I WILL REMEMBER YOU

Words and Music by
SARAH McLACHLAN, SEAMUS EGAN
and DAVE MERENDA

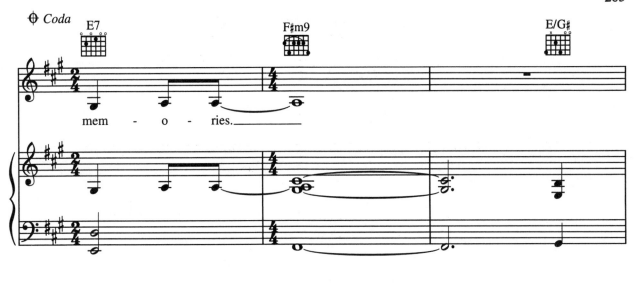

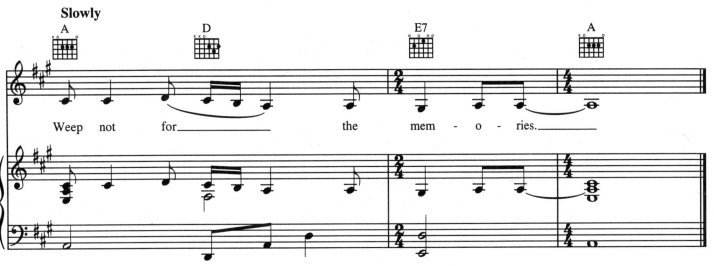

Verse 2:
So afraid to love you,
More afraid to lose.
I'm clinging to a past
That doesn't let me choose.
Where once there was a darkness,
A deep and endless night,
You gave me everything you had,
Oh, you gave me life.
(To Chorus:)

(Optional Verse 1 — Album version)
Remember the good times that we had,
I let them slip away from us when things got bad.
Now clearly I first saw you smiling in the sun.
I wanna feel your warmth upon me,
I wanna be the one.
(To Chorus:)

I'M YOUR ANGEL

Words and Music by
R. KELLY

Chorus:

IF I COULD TURN BACK THE HANDS OF TIME

Words and Music by
R. KELLY

Freely, with feeling

How did I ev-er let you slip a-way, nev-er know-ing I'd be sing-ing this song some-day? And now I'm

If I Could Turn Back the Hands of Time - 6 - 1

Vamp:
2. There'd be nothing I wouldn't do for you,
   Forever honest and true to you.
   If you accept me back in your heart, I love you.
3. Woah, that would be my will.
   Darlin', I'm begging you to take me by the hands.
4. I'm goin' down, yes, I am.
   Down on my bended knee, yeah.
   And I'm gonna be right there until you return to me.
5. Woah, if I could just turn back that little clock on the wall,
   Then I'd come to realize how much I love you.

IN THIS LIFE

Words and Music by
MIKE REID and ALLEN SHAMBLIN

Slowly ♩ = 63

1. For all I'd been blessed with in my life,_____
2. For ev-'ry moun-tain I have climbed,____

there was an emp-ti-ness in____ me.
ev-'ry rag-ing riv-er____ crossed,

In This Life - 4 - 1

IRONIC

Lyrics by
ALANIS MORISSETTE

Music by
ALANIS MORISSETTE
and GLEN BALLARD

Ironic - 6 - 1

think? A lit-tle too i-ron-ic... and yeah, I

real-ly do think... it's like rain _____ on your

wed-ding _____ day. It's a free ___ ride _____ when you're

al-read-y paid. It's the good ad-vice _____ that you

KILLING ME SOFTLY WITH HIS SONG

Words by
NORMAN GIMBEL

Music by
CHARLES FOX

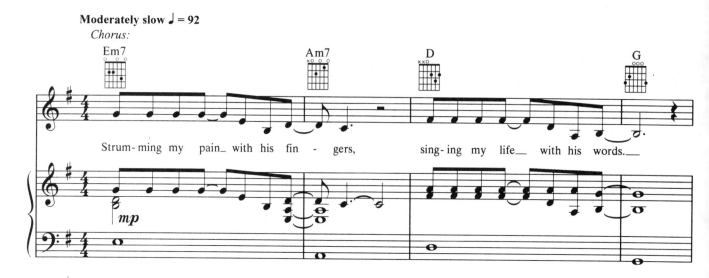

Killing Me Softly - 6 - 1

softly_____ with his song._____

Ooh,_____ do do do____ do do____ do.

Ooh,_____ do do do____ Ooh._____

230

Verse:
N.C.

1. I heard he sang___ a good___ song, I heard he had___ a style.___
2. I felt all flush___ with fe - ver, em - bar - rassed by___ the crowd.___

And so I came___ to see___ him to lis - ten___ for a while.___
I felt he found___ my let - ters and read each___ one out loud.___

And there he was___ this young___ boy, a stran - ger to___ my eyes.___
I prayed that he___ would fin - ish, but he just kept___ right on.___ }

Chorus:

2.
E
Em
Am7
Whoa, whoa.
D
G
Em7
Am7
La la la la la la, whoa,
D
C
G
C
la, whoa, la,
G/F
E
F
E
F
E
F
E
F
E
la.

KISS THE RAIN

Words and Music by
ERIC BAZILIAN, DESMOND CHILD
and BILLIE MYERS

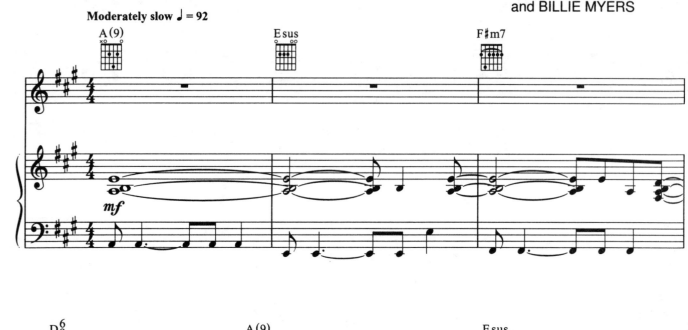

Kiss the Rain - 6 - 1

Kiss the Rain - 6 - 4

Verse 2:
Hello? Do you miss me?
I hear you say you do,
But not the way I'm missing you.
What's new? How's the weather?
Is it stormy where you are?
You sound so close,
But it feels like you're so far.
Oh, would it mean anything
If you knew what I'm left imagining
In my mind, in my mind.
Would you go, would you go...
(To Chorus:)

LARGER THAN LIFE

Words and Music by
MAX MARTIN, KRISTIAN LUNDIN
and BRIAN T. LITTRELL

242

Larger Than Life - 6 - 3

244

LOST IN YOUR EYES

Lyrics and Music by
TOM PETTY

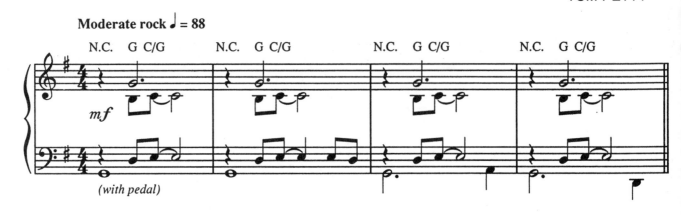

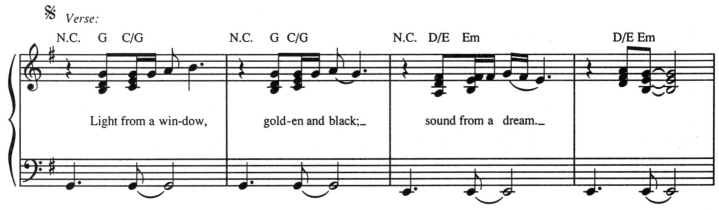

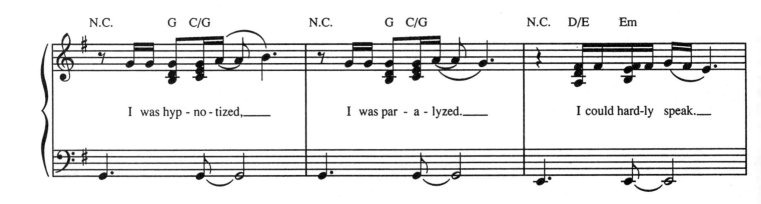

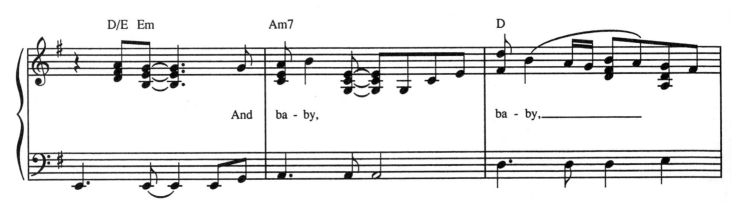

Lost in Your Eyes - 3 - 1

Verse 2:
Guess I understand it, guess I sort of have to,
Guess I kind of see.
Just because it could have been, doesn't mean it had to ever mean a thing.
And baby, baby, I could say it all the time, that . . .
(To Chorus:)

Verse 3:
Guess I understand it, guess I sort of have to,
Guess I kind of see.
Just because it could have been, doesn't mean it had to ever mean a thing.
And baby, baby, you never realized that . . .
(To Chorus:)

LOVE IS ALL AROUND

Words and Music by
REG PRESLEY

Love Is All Around - 5 - 1

250

Love Is All Around - 5 - 3

Verse 2:
I see your face before me
As I lay on my bed;
I cannot get to thinking
Of all the things you said.
You gave your promise to me
And I gave mine to you;
I need someone beside me
In everything I do.

IT'S ALL COMING BACK TO ME NOW

Words and Music by
JIM STEINMAN

1. There were

It's All Coming Back to Me Now - 8 - 1

256

It's All Coming Back to Me Now - 8 - 3

It's All Coming Back to Me Now - 8 - 8

MACARENA

Words and Music by
ANTONIO ROMERO
and RAFAEL RUIZ

Coro:

Da - le a tu cuer - po a-le-grí - a Ma-ca-re - na que tu cuer-po es pa' dar - le a-le-grí-a y co-sa bue-na.

Macarena - 6 - 1

Da - le a tu cuer - po a - le - grí - a Ma - ca - re - na, eh,_____ Ma - ca - re - na.

Verso 3:
Macarena sueña con el Corte inglés
Y se compra los modelos mas modernos.
Le gustaría vivir en Nueva York
Y ligar un novio nuevo.

Puente 2:
Macarena sueña con el Corte inglés
Y se compra los modelos mas modernos.
Le gustaría vivir en Nueva York
Y ligar un novio nuevo.
(Al Coro:)

Verso 4:
Macarena tiene un novio que se llama,
Que se llama de apellido Vitorino.
Y en la jura de bandera del muchacho
Se la dió con dos amigos.

Puente 3:
Macarena tiene un novio que se llama,
Que se llama de apellido Vitorino.
Y en la jura de bandera del muchacho
Se la dió con dos amigos.
(Al Coro:)

MISLED

Words and Music by
PETER ZIZZO and JIMMY BRALOWER

Rock ♩ = 112

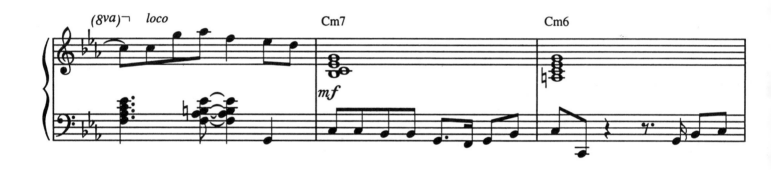

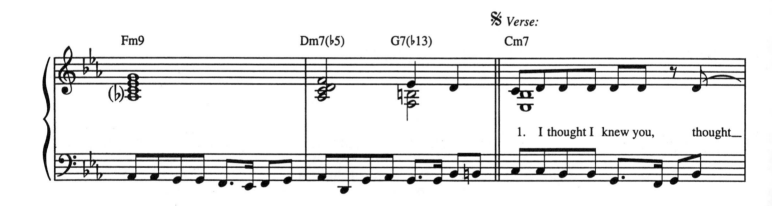

1. I thought I knew you, thought__

___ that I knew you well. We had a rhy-thm, but__ I guess you nev-er can tell.

Misled - 4 - 1

Cm7   Cm6   Fm9

Oh, I learned ear - ly nev - er to ig-nore the signs. You'll be for-giv - en, it

𝄋 𝄋 *Bridge:*

Dm7(♭5)   G7(♭13)   A♭maj7   E♭maj7

ain't worth that much to my mind. Lov-in' you (was) so eas - y, it's hard to say

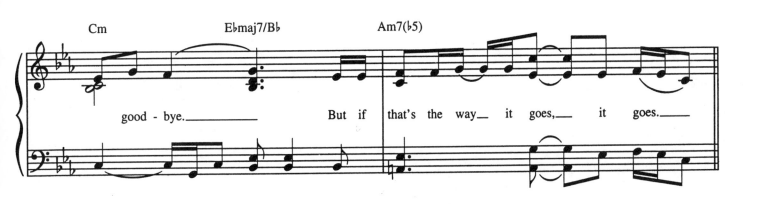

Cm   E♭maj7/B♭   Am7(♭5)

good - bye. But if that's the way it goes, it goes.

Chorus:

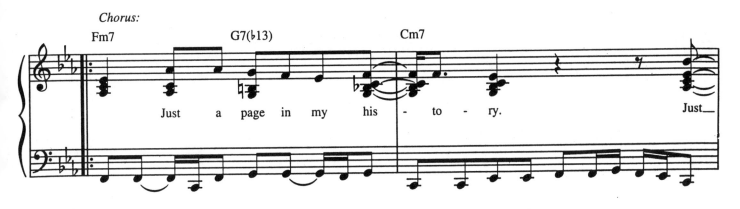

Fm7   G7(♭13)   Cm7

Just a page in my his - to - ry. Just

Misled - 4 - 2

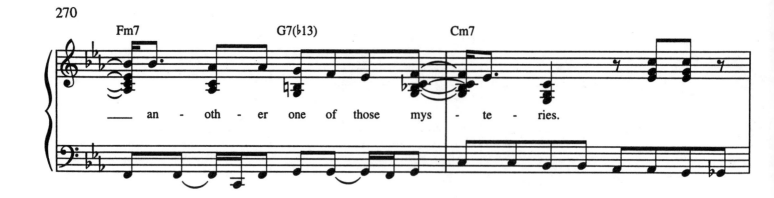

_____ an - oth - er one of those mys - te - ries.

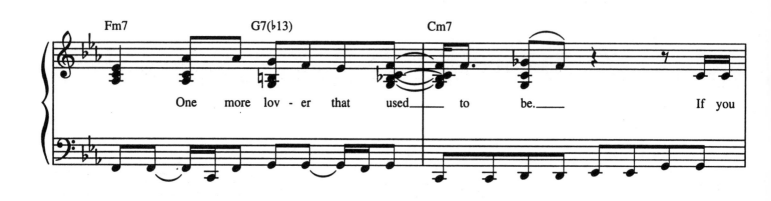

One more lov - er that used____ to be.____ If you

think you're in____ my head,____ you've been ser - i - ous - ly mis - led.

ser - i - ous - ly mis - led. ser - i - ous - ly mis - led.

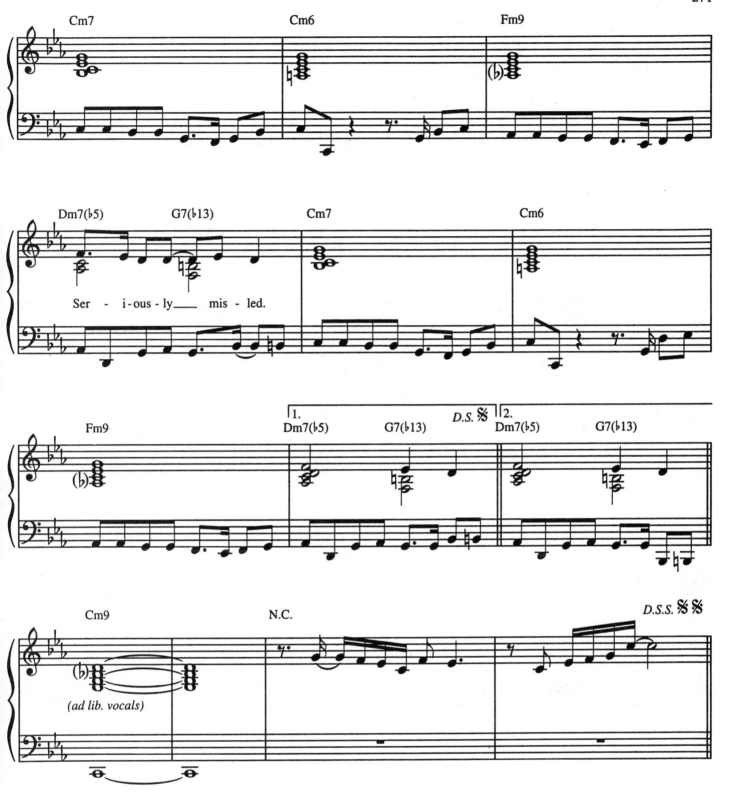

Verse 2:
Lovin' somebody ain't your average 9 to 5.
It takes conviction, it takes a will to survive.
I'm not somebody who commits the crime and leaves the scene.
But when I've been dissed, I don't spend much time on what might've been.

Bridges 2 & 3:
I'm not about self-pity, your love did me wrong,
So I'm movin', movin' on.
(To Chorus:)

NEVER EVER

Words by
SHAZNAY LEWIS

Music by
SHAZNAY LEWIS and RICKDY RAW

(Spoken) A few questions that I need to know, how you could ever hurt me so, I need to know what I've done wrong, and how long it's been going on. Was it that I never paid enough attention, or did I not give enough affection? Not only will your answers keep me sane, but I'll know never to make the same mistake again. You can tell me to my face

Never Ever - 6 - 1

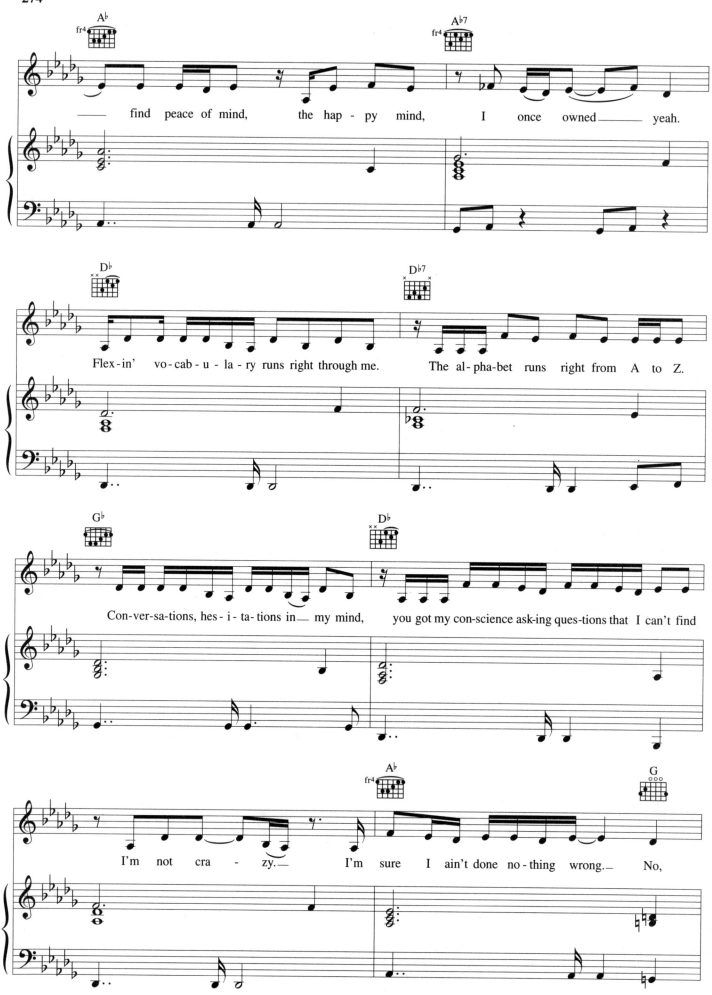

Never Ever - 6 - 4

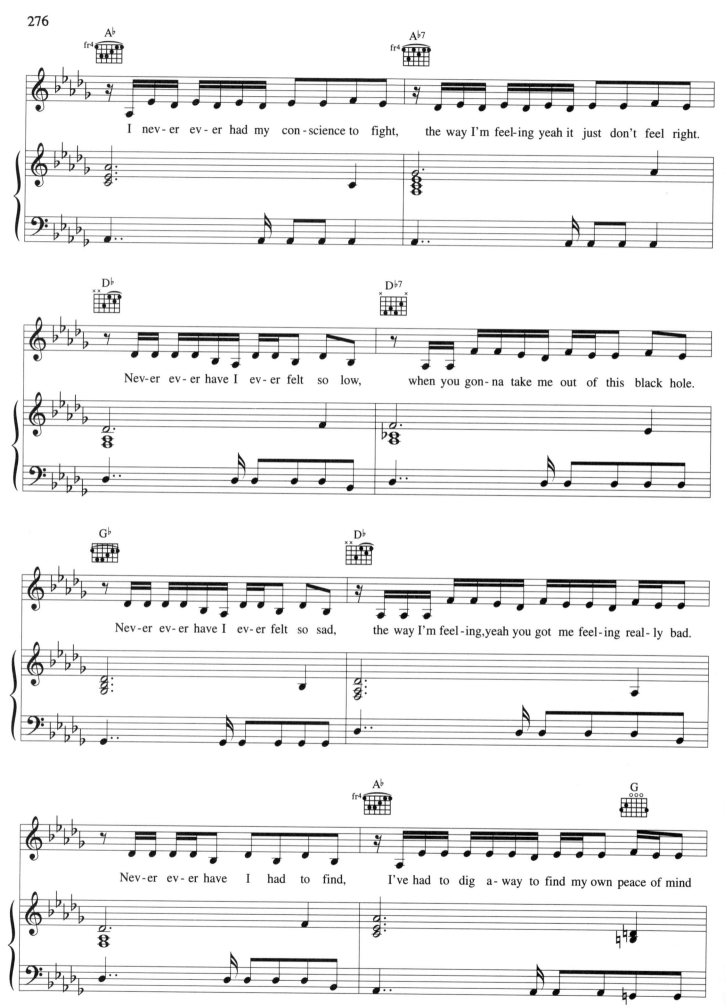

Verse 2:
I keep searching deep within my soul
For all the answers, don't wanna hurt no more.
I need peace, got to feel at ease, need to be
Free from pain, go insane, my heart aches.

Sometimes vocabulary runs through my head
The alphabet runs right from A to Z
Conversations, hesitations in my mind.
You got my conscience asking questions that I can't find
I'm not crazy
I'm sure I ain't done nothing wrong
Now I'm just waiting
'Cause I heard that this feeling won't last that long.

NO SCRUBS

Words and Music by
KEVIN BRIGGS, KANDI BURRIS
and TAMEKA COTTLE

Moderately ♩ = 100

Verse:

scrub is a guy that thinks__ he's fly and is al - so known as a bust - er.__

me. 2. *See additional lyrics*

No Scrubs - 6 - 1

Verse 2:
But a scrub is checkin' me,
But his game is kinda weak.
And I know that he can't approach me,
'Cause I'm lookin' like class and he's lookin' like trash.
'Can't get wit' no deadbeat ass. So
No, I don't want your number,
No, I don't want to give you mine,
No, I don't want to meet you nowhere,
No, I don't want none of your time.
And . . .
(To Chorus:)

NOW AND FOREVER

Music and Lyrics by
RICHARD MARX

Now and Forever - 4 - 1

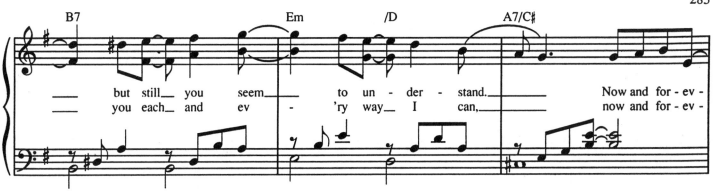

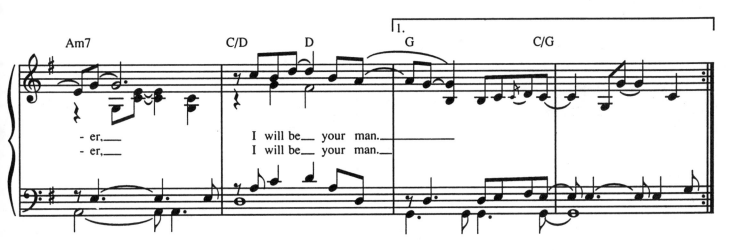

Now and Forever - 4 - 2

now and for ev - er,___ I will be___ your man.___

Now and for - ev - er,

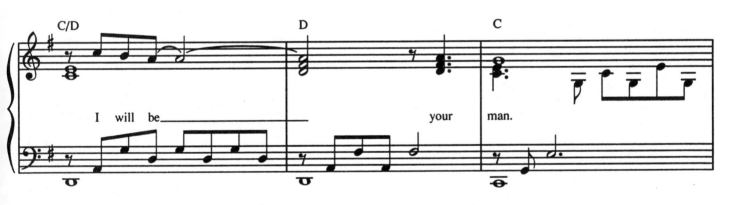

I will be___ your man.

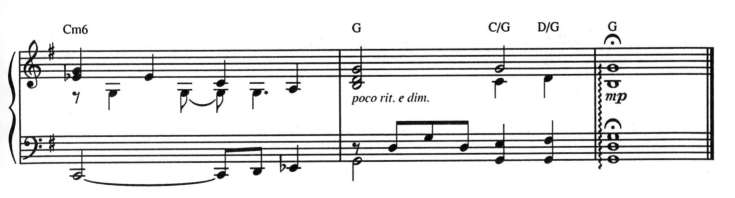

poco rit. e dim.

ONE OF US

Words and Music by
ERIC BAZILIAN

One of Us - 5 - 1

OPEN ARMS

Words and Music by
STEVE PERRY and
JONATHAN CAIN

Chorus:

come___ to you with o - pen arms,_ noth - ing to

hide,___ be - lieve what I say.___ So here___ I

To Coda

am___ with o - pen arms,_ hop - ing you see___ what your

love means to me;__ o - pen arms._____

296

QUIT PLAYING GAMES
(With My Heart)

Words and Music by
MAX MARTIN and HERBERT CRICHLOW

Verse 2:
I live my life the way,
To keep you comin' back to me.
Everything I do is for you,
So what is it that you can't see?
Sometimes I wish I could turn back time,
Impossible as it may seem.
But I wish I could so bad, baby
You better quit playing games with my heart.

RUN TO YOU

Words and Music by
JUD FRIEDMAN and ALLAN RICH

306

SAID I LOVED YOU . . . BUT I LIED

Composed by
MICHAEL BOLTON and
ROBERT JOHN "MUTT" LANGE

Said I Loved You . . . But I Lied - 5 - 1

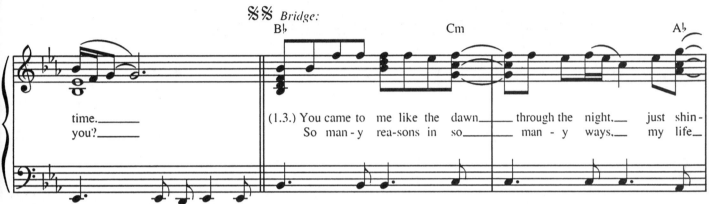

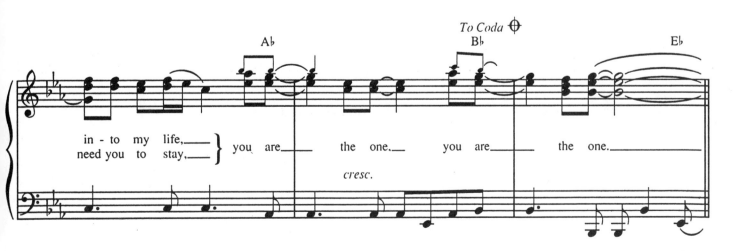

Said I Loved You . . . But I Lied - 5 - 2

feel___ in - side.___ Said I___ loved you, but I was wrong,___

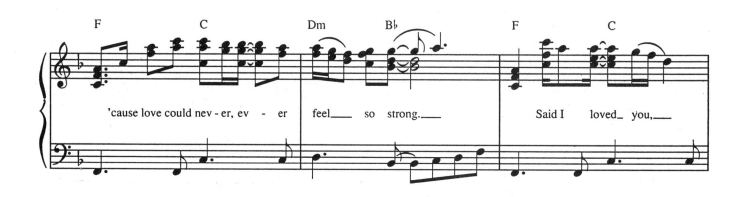

'cause love could nev - er, ev - er feel___ so strong.___ Said I loved_ you,___

'cause this is more than love_ I feel___ in - side.___

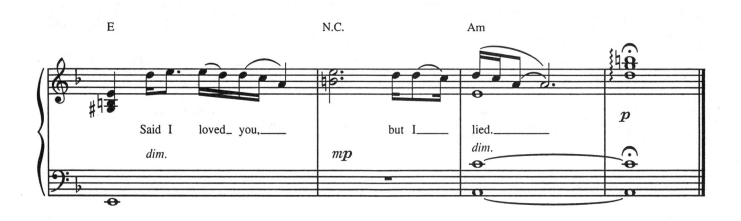

Said I loved_ you,___ but I___ lied.___

Save The Best For Last

Words and Music by
WENDY WALDMAN, JON LIND
and PHIL GALDSTON

Save the Best for Last - 5 - 1

316

the best for last.

Some-times the ver-y thing you're look-

ing for is the one thing you can't see. Some-times the snow

SHAKE YOUR BON-BON

Words and Music by
ROBI ROSA, GEORGE NORIEGA
and DESMOND CHILD

— are you my Ju - li - et?___ I feel a mad con - nec - tion with your bo - dy.

Shake your bon - bon, Shake your bon - bon, Shake your bon - bon.

I wan-na be your lov - er,___ your on -ly La - tin lov - er.___

We'll go 'round the world_ in a da - ay.___ Don't say no, no,

Shake it my way, oh, Shake your bon - bon, Shake your bon - bon, Shake your bon - bon.

Verse

2. You're a Mat - a Ha - ri,___ I wan - na know your sto - ry,___

In the Sa - ha - ra sun,___ I wan - na be the one___ who's gon - na come and take you, make you

shake your bon - bon, Shake your bon - bon, Shake your bon - bon. Up in the Him - a - la -

SOMETIMES

Words and Music by
JÖRGEN ELOFSSON

Bridge:

From the Original Motion Picture Soundtrack "REALITY BITES"
STAY (I MISSED YOU)

Words and Music by
LISA LOEB

*Gtr. should capo 1st fret if matching the original recording key of D♭.

Stay (I Missed You) - 6 - 1

I thought_ that I was strong._____ I thought,_ "Hey, I can leave,_ I can leave."_

But now I know that I____ was wrong 'cause I missed you.

I missed you._____

You said, "You caught me 'cause you want me and one day I'll let you go." You try to

STAY THE SAME

Words and Music by
JOEY McINTYRE and JOE CARRIER

338

340

STREETS OF PHILADELPHIA

Words and Music by
BRUCE SPRINGSTEEN

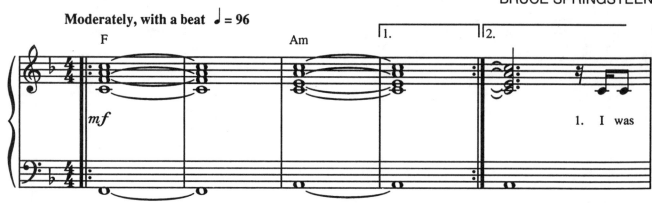

Moderately, with a beat ♩ = 96

1. I was

Verse:

bruised and bat-tered; I could-n't __ tell __ what I felt. I was __ un-rec-og-niz - a-ble __ to my-

self. Saw my re-flec-tion in a win-dow and did-n't know my own face. __ Oh, broth-er are you

gon-na leave me wast-in' a - way on the streets of Phil-a - del-phi-a. __
(bkgrd.) La __ la la la la

(L.H. cue notes 2nd & 3rd time)

Streets of Philadelphia - 3 - 1

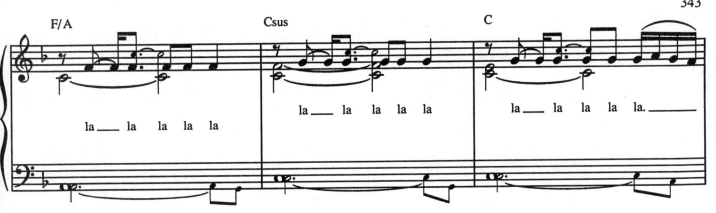

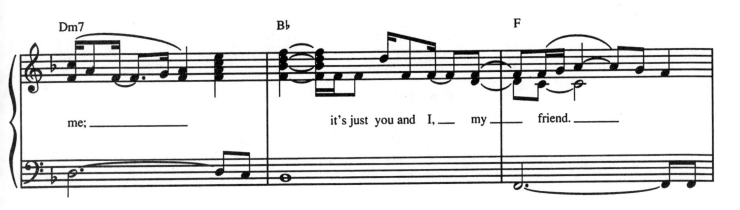

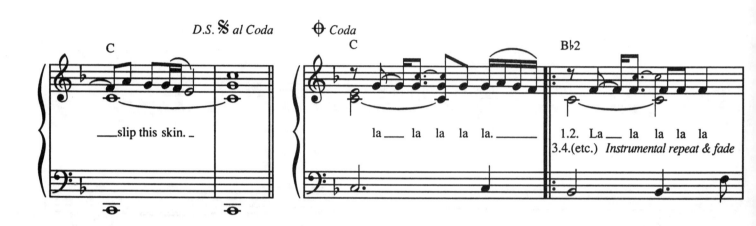

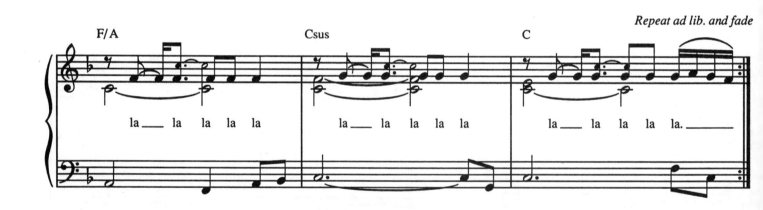

Verse 2:
I walked the avenue till my legs felt like stone.
I heard the voices of friends vanished and gone.
At night I could hear the blood in my veins
Just as black and whispering as the rain
On the streets of Philadelphia.
(To Chorus:)

Verse 3:
The night has fallen. I'm lyin' awake.
I can feel myself fading away.
So, receive me, brother, with your faithless kiss,
Or will we leave each other alone like this
On the streets of Philadelphia?
(To Chorus:)

THAT DON'T IMPRESS ME MUCH

Words and Music by
SHANIA TWAIN and R.J. LANGE

That Don't Impress Me Much - 5 - 1

Verse 2:
I never knew a guy who carried a mirror in his pocket
And a comb up his sleeve, just in case.
And all that extra hold gel in your hair oughtta lock it,
'Cause heaven forbid it should fall outta place.
Oh, oh, you think you're special.
Oh, oh, you think you're something else.
(Spoken:) OK, so you're Brad Pitt.
(To Chorus:)

Verse 3:
You're one of those guys who likes to shine his machine.
You make me take off my shoes before you let me get in.
I can't believe you kiss your car good-night.
Come on, baby, tell me, you must be jokin', right?
Oh, oh, you think you're special.
Oh, oh, you think you're something else.
(Spoken:) OK, so you've got a car.
(To Chorus:)

SUNNY CAME HOME

Words and Music by
SHAWN COLVIN and JOHN LEVENTHAL

Sunny Came Home - 6 - 1

352

354

THAT GIRL

Words and Music by
GARY BENSON, MAXI ELLIOT, ROBERT LIVINGSTON,
ORVILLE BURRELL, BOOKER T. JONES, STEVE CROPPER,
DONALD DUNN and AL JACKSON

That Girl - 5 - 1

360

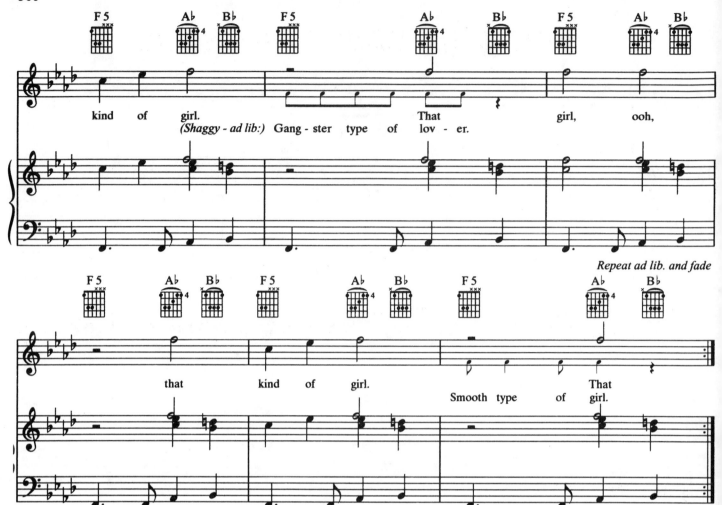

Bridge 2:
That girl to make you break your silence and speak.
Just a glimpse upon the silhouette makes my knees get weak.
Baby, baby, so unique, a reggaematic,
Lover, lover, make her life complete.
(To Chorus:)

Bridge 3:
Well, I'm weak to her touch,
So vulnerable to her blush, love struck.
That girl, I got an instant crush.
You can call me a lush, infatuation or just lust.
The girl possess the stuff to make the man, then, oh, ah...
(To Chorus:)

Shaggy's ad-lib:
Gangster kind of lover,
'Cause she's the shaggy kind of girl.
I got to let them know.
Sexy kind of lover,
Maxi kind of girl.
I got to let them know,
She's the kind of girl that captivates your soul.
A rude girl type of love.
Shaggy and Maxi Priest definitely on the girl them case.

WHO WILL SAVE YOUR SOUL

Words and Music by
JEWEL KILCHER

Moderate shuffle feel ♩ = 112

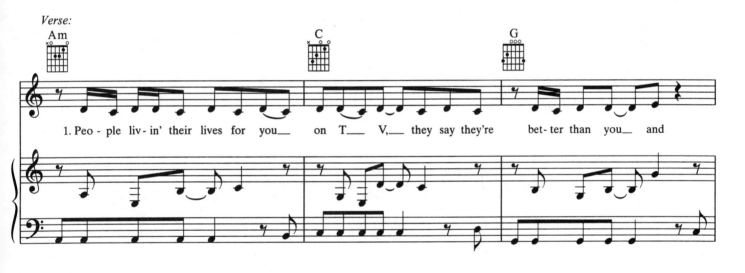

1. Peo - ple liv - in' their lives for you__ on T__ V,__ they say they're bet - ter than you__ and

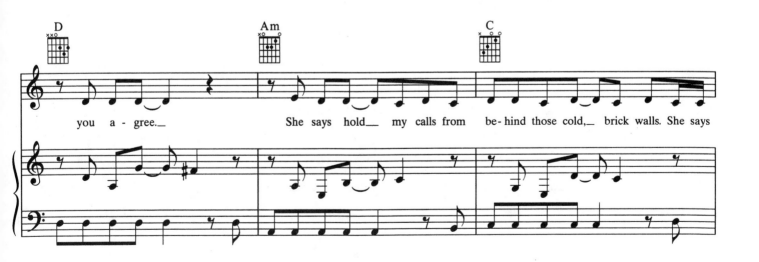

you a - gree.__ She says hold__ my calls from be - hind those cold,__ brick walls. She says

Who Will Save Your Soul - 7 - 1

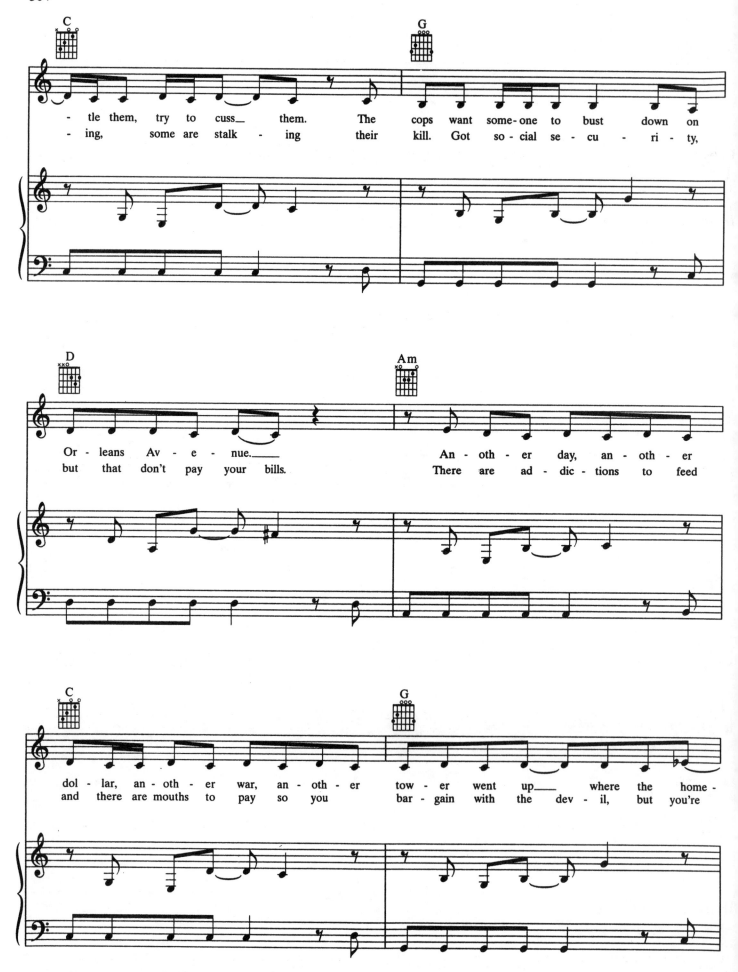

Chorus:

WALKIN' ON THE SUN

Words and Music by
STEVE HARWELL, GREGORY CAMP,
PAUL DeLISLE and KEVIN COLEMAN

Walkin' on the Sun - 6 - 1

372

Walkin' on the Sun - 6 - 5

Verse 2:
Twenty-five years ago they spoke out
And they broke out of recession and oppression.
And together they toked and they folked out with guitars
Around a bonfire, just singin' and clappin'; man, what the hell happened?
Yeah, some were spellbound, some were hell bound,
Some, they fell down and some got back up and fought back against the meltdown.
And their kids were hippie chicks, all hypocrites
Because their fashion is smashin' the true meaning of it.
(To Chorus:)

WHEREVER YOU GO

Words and Music by
DURELL BOTTOMS, NICOLE RENEE
and MICHAEL McCRARY

1. Since you left___ me,___ my life

2. *See additional lyrics*

Wherever You Go - 6 - 1

376

Wherever You Go - 6 - 3

Bridge:

Verse 2:
Goodbye is such a hard thing to say
When you're wrong, I know,
When you're my everything.
And who will stay and care for me?
When you're gone, I'll be all alone.
Who will come and comfort me
And fulfill my needs?
Who will love me?
Who will care?
Who will be there
When I need someone for me?
Who will be there
When I go down on my knees?
I need you to say, . . .
(To Chorus:)

From the Motion Picture "BOYS ON THE SIDE"

YOU GOT IT

Words and Music by
ROY ORBISON, JEFF LYNNE
and TOM PETTY

382

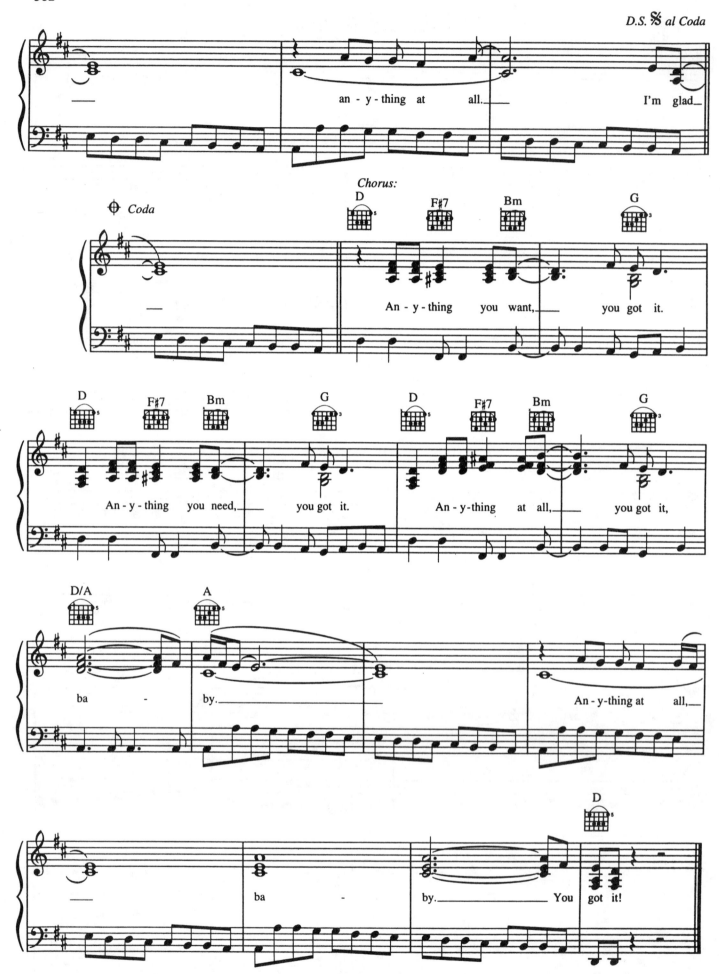

You Got It - 3 - 3

YOU LEARN

Lyrics by
ALANIS MORISSETTE

Music by
ALANIS MORISSETTE
and GLEN BALLARD

I _____ rec-om-mend get-ting your heart tram-pled on to
I _____ rec-om-mend bit-ing off more than you can chew to

an-y-one, yeah. _____
an-y-one, I _____ cer-tain-ly do.

You Learn - 5 - 1

YOU MUST LOVE ME

Words by
TIM RICE

Music by
ANDREW LLOYD WEBBER

feel - ing   fright - ened you'll slip   a - way,   you must   love

me,   you must   love   me.

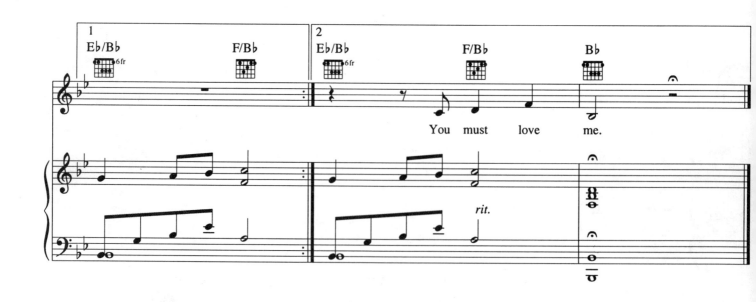

You must   love   me.

Additional Lyrics

Verse 2: *(Instrumental 8 bars)*
Why are you at my side?
How can I be any use to you now?
Give me a chance and I'll let you see how
Nothing has changed.
Deep in my heart I'm concealing
Things that I'm longing to say,
Scared to confess what I'm feeling
Frightened you'll slip away,
You must love me.

YOU'RE STILL THE ONE

Words and Music by
SHANIA TWAIN and R.J. LANGE

You're Still the One - 3 - 1

392

Verse 2:
Ain't nothin' better,
We beat the odds together.
I'm glad we didn't listen.
Look at what we would be missin'.
(To Bridge:)

COME TO MY WINDOW

Words and Music by
MELISSA ETHERIDGE

Come to My Window - 4 - 1

Verse 2:
Keeping my eyes open, I cannot afford to sleep.
Giving away promises I know that I can't keep.
Nothing fills the blackness that has seeped into my chest.
I need you in my blood, I am forsaking all the rest.
Just to reach you,
Just to reach you.
Oh, to reach you.
(To Chorus:)

The Best Personality Folios of 1999

CHRISTINA AGUILERA
(PF9927) Piano/Vocal/Chords

BACKSTREET BOYS
(PF9731A) Piano/Vocal/Chords
Millennium
(PF9916) Piano/Vocal/Chords

GARTH BROOKS
Double Live
(PF9906) Piano/Vocal/Chords

CELINE DION
All The Way... A Decade of Song
(0437B) Piano/Vocal/Chords
Let's Talk About Love
(PF9813) Piano/Vocal/Chords

JEWEL
Spirit
(PF9836) Piano/Vocal/Chords
(PG9810) Guitar/Vocal with Tablature

KID ROCK
Devil Without A Cause
(0422B) Authentic Guitar-Tab Edition

KORN
Issues
(PGM0001) Authentic Guitar-Tab Edition

LIMP BIZKIT
Three Dollar Bill
(PG9901) Authentic Guitar-Tab Edition

LIVE
The Distance to Here
(PG9911) Authentic Guitar-Tab Edition

*NSYNC
(PF9908) Piano/Vocal/Chords

RAGTIME
Vocal Selections
(5206A) Piano/Vocal/Chords

SANTANA
Supernatural
(0413B) Authentic Guitar-Tab Edition

BRITNEY SPEARS
...Baby One More Time
(PF9911) Piano/Vocal/Chords

STAR WARS
Episode I: The Phantom Menace
(0347B) Piano/Vocal/Chords

SHANIA TWAIN
Come on Over
(PF9746) Piano/Vocal/Chords

KENNY WAYNE SHEPARD
Live On
(PG9909) Authentic Guitar-Tab Edition